Minimalist Living
Made Easy

Simon Davies

Text Copyright © Simon Davies

All rights reserved. No part of this guide may be reproduced in any form without permission in writing from the publisher except in the case of brief quotations embodied in critical articles or reviews.

Legal & Disclaimer

The information contained in this book and its contents is not designed to replace or take the place of any form of medical or professional advice; and is not meant to replace the need for independent medical, financial, legal or other professional advice or services, as may be required. The content and information in this book have been provided for educational and entertainment purposes only.

The content and information contained in this book have been compiled from sources deemed reliable, and it is accurate to the best of the Author's knowledge, information, and belief. However, the Author cannot guarantee its accuracy and validity and cannot be held liable for any errors and/or omissions. Further, changes are periodically made to this book as and when needed. Where appropriate and/or necessary, you must consult a professional (including but not limited to your doctor, attorney, financial advisor or such other professional advisor) before using any of the suggested remedies, techniques, or information in this book.

Upon using the contents and information contained in this book, you agree to hold harmless the Author from and against any damages, costs, and expenses, including any legal fees potentially resulting from the application of any of the information provided by this book. This disclaimer applies to any loss, damages or injury caused by the use and application, whether directly or indirectly, of any advice or information presented, whether for breach of contract, tort, negligence, personal injury, criminal intent, or under any other cause of action.

You agree to accept all risks of using the information presented inside this book.

You agree that by continuing to read this book, where appropriate and/or necessary, you shall consult a professional (including but not limited to your doctor, attorney, or financial advisor or such other advisor as needed) before using any of the suggested remedies, techniques, or information in this book.

Contents

Introduction 1

Chapter 1: What Is Minimalism And How It All Started 3

1.1 What Is Minimalism Living, What Does It Entail 5

1.2 What Is The Purpose Of Minimalism? 12

Chapter 2: Are You A Minimalist? 15

2.1 What Does It Mean To Be A Minimalist? 18

2.2 Common Misconceptions About Minimalism 25

Chapter 3: Dealing With Clutter In Life 30

3.1 How Decluttering Changes Your Life 33

Chapter 4: Minimalism In Different Areas Of Life 38

4.1 Essential Relationship 39

4.2 Parenting 49

4.3 Career Life 54

4.4 Finances 61

Chapter 5: Needs & Wants 66

5.1 What Is The Difference Between Things You Need & Things You Want 68

5.2 How To Identify The Thing You Need From Things You Want 70

5.3 How To Distinguish The Differences Between The Two That Promote Minimalism 73

Chapter 6: Optimizing Life For Minimalism 76

6.1 A Simple Plan For Home Declutter 79

6.2 Decluttering Your Home 82

6.3 Decluttering Your Material Possessions 102

6.4 Decluttering Your Gadgets 110

6. 5 Decluttering Your Schedule 121

Chapter 7: A Life Of Abundance 136

Chapter 8: Minimalism Maintenance 144

8.1 Ways To Maintain Your Minimalist Lifestyle Permanently 147

8.2 Common Items To Never Buy If You Want To Have A Clutter-Free Home 152

8.3 Fighting The Desire 156

Conclusion 158

Introduction

The truth is, no one wakes up and says, "Oh, I want to start a minimalist lifestyle starting today." No one simply falls for it. For many, it takes years and losing good relationships and career before they realize that there is a toxic in their life they needed to get rid of.

This was the case for me.

For years, I let my life out of control, which affected my relationship, my career, and even social life negatively – everything seemed so rampant. I know it was my fault; everything was just a result of my own doing. But it came to a point that I had enough – every bad thing must come to an end.

When I discovered minimalism lifestyle, I was able to turn my life around and direct it to a more organized, pleasant life.

Anyone can live a minimalist life. I believe that your life is not set in stone and anyone can improve or change.

All the choices and decisions you make about the quality of your life are laid out based on the simplicity or complexity of your decisions.

In this book, I want to share how life-changing minimalism can be and how to do it right. And hopefully, it can help you take back control over your life and direct you to the path of contentment.

Furthermore, this book is also meant to help you develop new skills and discover hobbies that you didn't think you would like. Basically, you will learn the basics of having fun and enjoying life for what it really has to offer. This will also help you become more appreciative of the basics of living, without unnecessary expensive materialistic things, which frees up your mind, and lets you find your purpose and eventually, allows you to become a calmer, happier, and more loving individual.

Chapter 1

WHAT IS MINIMALISM AND HOW IT ALL STARTED

It has been long debated within the design community as to when exactly, minimalism first came about. Some people believe that it all started in the middle of the Modernist movement during the early 20th century when new materials like steel, glass, and concrete were starting to become widely available. On the other hand, some argue that it really started much later, as an extension of the Minimalist art movement during the 1960s to 1970s, when artists like Ellsworth Kelly and Donald Judd turned back from Abstract Expressionism supporting next level abstractions which includes simple geometric shapes.

In spite of its blurred timeline, minimalism has been – and continues to be –one of the most powerful movements of the 20th and 21st centuries throughout the world of architecture, art, product design, and lifestyle. A response against excess, the goal of this Zen-like approach is to show the beauty of simplicity, elegance, and utility by getting rid of things that might be unnecessary.

Today, minimalism is usually associated with Japanese traditional Zen-style design and home organization approach (thanks to Marie Kondo's show on Netflix that influenced many all over the world to discard any item in their home that does not "spark joy"). Zen style design and art focus on getting rid of any unnecessary add-ons or decorations. These arts are usually referred to as aesthetics of elimination as they allow endless beauty and profusion occur from less, instead of more. Huge creative power is used into recognizing and eliminating all unnecessary things, whether it is an element, space, shapes, colour, decoration, and even habits.

1.1 What Is Minimalism Living, What Does It Entail

Just like on many other "trends" it's quite unfortunate that a lot of people go all-out towards being minimalist, even if they actually have no idea what a minimalist lifestyle truly entails. For some, living a minimalist lifestyle means living in an isolated place. And while for others, it could mean living a luxurious life.

What is it really about?

Have you ever had an empty cupboard or cabinet space in your home? Chances are you have had the urge to find or even buy something you can put in it to just fill it up and give it a "purpose." But have you really given enough thought if the thing you are going to put in it has a purpose? While your cupboard or cabinet space is there for a reason, it shouldn't be necessary to use them unless you really needed to. Do you really need to buy a dozen piece of tableware even if you live alone just to fill in your cupboard? Or do you really need to buy that swan figurine just to have something to put on your cabinet display space? Those are just unnecessary clutters!

Living a minimalist lifestyle means living only with things you really use and need. This is not to say that becoming a minimalist means having to spend less money; this simply means living a life that makes you spend money only on things that you actually need.

Aside from having a lot of unnecessary things, a lot of people lack contentment in life. Wanting to attain success quickly would not guarantee the happiness you might be looking for; it would rather continue to make life a lot harder than what it already is.

Living a minimalist lifestyle involves being content with how your life already is as long as you're healthy and your basic needs are met. But this doesn't mean it's unnecessary to want a better life, a better body, or a better job – there's always room for improvement, you don't have to be unhappy just because you haven't had the better version of yourself or your life just yet.

A lot of people find it difficult to be content, maybe because it's so easy to compare your life to others', which can be really toxic. Living a minimalist life, on the other hand, is focusing on what you already have and making the best out of it.

It takes time

Being a successful minimalist takes a huge amount of change in your life, as well as routine and your way of thinking.

While a lot of people associate minimalism with reducing the number of your possessions, it's just not about that. In fact, minimalism is more about reducing the things that are holding you back, things that consume a lot of your time, which make you inefficient on a regular basis.

Minimalism also has something to do with a change of mindset. It's a lot more about the individual, the feelings, and experiences rather than about your physical possessions.

It is the process of changing your life entirely that takes time and is not just about getting rid of your things in your house. It is a process that involves accepting and knowing that many things are essentially holding you back.

It shows how spending more of your time with people and enduring different experiences rather than shopping and spending money will have more of an incredible effect on your life. Unlike some fundamental life-changing courses or methods, the benefits you will get from minimalism may take some time to take effect and become obvious. But then again, trusting the process is a part of the whole idea of minimalism.

Minimalism is intentionality

It's marked by purpose, clarity, as well as intentionality. At its very core, minimalism is the intentional highlighting of the things that are important to us and the elimination of the stuff that distracts us from it. It's a lifestyle that attracts intentionality. And therefore, it attracts improvements in most parts of your life.

Minimalism is freedom from physical possessions

Today's culture has made us believe that a good life can be found by accruing things – by having as many things as we can. Many of us think that the more things we have, the better, which gives us this kind of idea that happiness can be bought at a shopping store.

But having a good life is not about having more things.

Minimalism helps us have freedom from the all-consuming desire to possess everything. It drags us off consumerism and encourages us to seek happiness elsewhere. It helps us give importance to experiences, relationships, healthcare, and soul-care.

Minimalism is freedom from modern hysteria

We live in a feverish pace of life. Many of us seem to be rushed, hurried, and stressed. We tend to work at passionate hours just to pay the bill as if working is the only thing we are meant to do. We rush to doing one activity to another or even multitasking while doing so, but at the end of the day, still not finding the satisfaction of getting things done. We keep ourselves in close connection with others through the internet, but real life-changing relationships carry on eluding us.

Minimalism helps us slow our life down and keeps us free from this modern mania to live faster. It gives us the opportunity to find the freedom to disengage. It seeks to highlight only life's essentials. It pursues to get rid of the frivolous and keep the only things that are important. And throughout the process, it values the intentional undertakings that overall, add value to life.

Minimalism is freedom from deception

Even though no one purposely chooses it, a lot of us live in deception. We live one life with our family, one with our co-workers, and another one with our neighbors. The lifestyle we have requires us to render a specific external image depending on the situation.

On the other hand, a simple life is ruled by unity and consistency. It is a form of lifestyle that's entirely transferable regardless of what the situation is. This means not looking at Friday night and Monday morning differently.

Minimalism is counter-cultural

We live in a society that is heavily influenced by celebrities. We see them on TV, read about them in magazines, and even follow them on social media. Their lives are envied by many, and many wish they lived the same way these celebrities do. People who are living a minimalist lifestyle are not impressed by the media correspondingly. A minimalist doesn't fit into the culture of consumerism that's endorsed by corporations and influential people. Yet, they're living a life that's pretty inviting and attractive.

While a lot of people are racing to acquire glamour, success, and reputation, minimalism can be recognized with a quieter, smaller, and calmer voice. It encourages us to consume less, slow down, and enjoy more.

Minimalism is completely achievable

Anyone can be a minimalist. As long as you are open to embracing an intentional lifestyle of living with less and leave your old lifestyle forever, you can be successful at it.

1.2 What Is The Purpose Of Minimalism?

A minimalist lifestyle is a life that demands the best of it by getting rid of the things that instead of making your life fun and fulfilling, making it more difficult and miserable.

Today, more and more people are starting to see the rewards they can get if they choose to live with less stuff. But again, what you have to keep in mind is that minimalism is not about being cheap or compromising your basic comforts for the sake of some principled religious philosophy. It is not even close to that. It is simply a choice fortified by the desire to reduce your possessions and to choose to live a simpler life with simpler intention.

You no longer want to be part of the dizzying rat-race of the 21st century's consumer world. Many people may have different definitions of minimalism, but the main idea of this lifestyle is to help you. Here are some of the things you can do when looking to change to a minimalist lifestyle:

- ❖ Be free from excess stuff
- ❖ Chase your passions
- ❖ Contribute beyond yourself
- ❖ Create more and consume less
- ❖ Determine your missions
- ❖ Discover your life purpose
- ❖ Eliminate your dissatisfaction
- ❖ Experience freedom
- ❖ Pay attention to your health
- ❖ Grow as a person
- ❖ Live in the moment
- ❖ Make the most of your time

By following the minimalist lifestyle, you will be able to finally find lasting happiness – and isn't that what each one of us is looking for? All of us want to be happy and most of us think that having everything – power, material things, recognition, etc. – is what going to make us truly happy. The purpose of minimalism is to help us realize these things are worthless if seen from the perspective of someone who knows what genuine happiness feels like.

Chapter 2

Are You A Minimalist?

What makes minimalist individuals different from those who are not? Here are some typical signs or traits you may develop as you live your life following the minimalist lifestyle.

You see depth within simplicity

Within every item that you have, the experiences you get, and even with people you meet, you will start to see an underlying emphasis on their functionality and purpose. It's like when you look at something, the first thought you have is "This can be very useful for me," instead of "This will look good in my living room."

You see organizing every part of your life with a therapeutic appeal

You either live a ploddingly well-ordered life or aspire to be. Making a list is something you love to do: must-do lists, grocery lists, goal lists, all the lists! As soon as you thought of an idea or a plan, you immediately feel empowered, and even the hardest tasks seem to be doable.

You seek for everything to look good together all the time, but you don't make a fuss about your looks

Unless you have been invited to a party, you're likely not to be seen dressed up to the nines. No matter what the occasion is, you'd always rather comfortable clothing and look natural. Again, simplicity is what you live for.

You appreciate quality and the finer things, and get little to no satisfaction from cheaper alternatives

While you might still think that it's a good idea to save some money, you'd rather be spending $500 on a high-quality appliance that may last for years, instead of buying a $50 one that even though may look exactly the same, you cannot guarantee the quality of it. You have a great appreciation for fine quality and craftsmanship and you feel the more of a purpose it has, the better.

You find cleanliness and functionality more appealing than the overly decorative

Your space is more valued and you'd prefer sit on the floor like how Japanese people would instead of filling up every inch of your house with things that don't have any functionality and purpose. This is not to say that your home is expected to be dull and lacking in personality. In fact, for many, it's the other way around – it simply means that you choose all your stuff carefully. Your home becomes an evident extension of your personality.

Cleaning becomes a hobby for you rather than a chore

It becomes a norm for you to pick out things that are not in their right places and put them where they should be in the first place. Clearing out the superfluous brings you a sense of fulfillment as well as simplifying your life and re-evaluating your priorities.

Your loathing to clutter extends to the people you encounter every day

You are very picky about whom you spend your time with and the people you interact with. So, you probably find yourself cleaning out your Facebook friend list from time to time as well!

Like many popular "trends", there are going to be inadequate knockoffs that don't hold up the values of a successful minimalist. On the other hand, once these traits are applied systematically and considerately, this lifestyle can leave you with powerful lasting benefits that go beyond sheer visuals.

2.1 What Does It Mean To Be A Minimalist?

Regardless of the hype around minimalism, it's quite obvious that many people still get a wrong impression of it. Again, it's not just about limiting the number of your possessions and living far from the comfort offered by the modern world.

And while such extreme forms of minimalism do exist, there are much milder forms of this lifestyle, some of which that still provide all the benefits a minimalist life can bring but doesn't require you to sell all the things you own and live in a 90-square-foot box in the middle of nowhere. Minimalism is by no means a radical change of lifestyle, but instead an optimal one.

Minimalism isn't a set of rules.

Because there are no strict rules you have to follow, the idea of minimalism may come in different for different people. For some, it might only be about getting rid of physical possessions and decluttering their homes, while for others, it is more about getting rid of unnecessary thoughts, beliefs, and even people.

To illustrate this diversity, we asked different people living a minimalist life to explain what minimalism means for them.

"For me, minimalism is living deliberately and considerately of the environment, ourselves, and those around us. It means removing (and then not re-accumulating) things in life that we don't use or need.

In my life, that means ridding myself of the "stuff" of life that begins to accumulate and overwhelm me, being intentional about purchases, and diminishing waste and clutter." — *Mary Spires (Accountant)*

"Minimalism is my rebellion against consumerism. I'm tired of buying things because I'm supposed to have the latest new style or makeup trend. I want to save money and only buy what I truly love or need. I never want to go into debt like my parents did. It makes me feel calmer and more in tune with what I actually own instead of feeling ingratitude." — *Lilly Sander (Librarian)*

"Being able to let go... not just of things but of associating things with people and memories. After being an only child, the oldest granddaughter, and only great-granddaughter/granddaughter to have any children on my side... everything has been passed down to me for my kids, apparently.

At 35, I am the matriarch of the family and the only one with children to carry in our family. So, what? It means everything is now in my home and basement that was my family owned. I have had to take baby steps to let it go. I'm only starting this journey. The courier cabinet that my grandfather made my grandmother 100 years ago for their first wedding anniversary... my grandmother's hope chest... my mother's wedding dress... I am having a hard time letting it all go but piece by piece, I am coming to terms that the stuff is not my mother, grandmother, and great grandmother... I will keep some of it, but I honor them every day being a good mom to my 3 young children, not by stashing their stuff away in my basement." — *Elizabeth Kerns (Teacher)*

"For me, minimalism is item curation. I feel like I don't see minimalists writing enough about how cool and valuable stuff can be. Stuff gets a bad rap in minimalism. I like buying things. I like researching things to buy. I like thinking of ways that I can buy something cool and unique to replace one or a couple of the things I already own.

I obsess over stuff. If you have just the right stuff, you don't need any other stuff. I have 5 shirts, 3 pants, a pair of jeans, and 6 shirts. Each and every piece was lovingly picked out and I have fun picking them out. It seems like most people achieve minimalism by caring about things less. I achieved it by caring about things more. Minimalism is a hobby for me. Yes, it takes time and effort to curate a beautiful list of objects, but it takes time and effort to practice any hobby." — ***Ricky Manning (Mathematician)***

"I think everyone is different, it is a lifestyle that adapts to you and your needs. There is no 'one size fits all' approach to minimalism.

We are a family of four that travel worldwide full time, world schooling our kids as we go, being able to really immerse ourselves in new cultures and languages. We are a family of minimalists, we have one carry on size suitcase each and that is all. We have what we need, we have clothes, depending on the country depends on what we have; we spent 18 months in hot and sunny countries so we only had short stops. This winter we went where there was snow, so we had thermals, jumpers, and coats. I think the key for us is not holding onto things that we do not need. When we change climates, we change what we own; the kids outgrow their clothes each season which makes this easier. We do not get too attached to the 'stuff' because that is all it is 'stuff' – things that can be replaced.

Our adventures and experiences, time spent together creating memories, that is what living is all about. We have all our toiletries, we have our devices, a couple phones, a couple laptops as we work remotely online, and a couple kindles for our children as they LOVE to read, and books are SO heavy. The children have a few toys each and a favorite teddy. When we are going to be choosing a place for a few months we buy extras for the kids, in Costa Rica we had a pool, so we bought some cool inflatable pool toys while we there. When we leave we leave them for the next guests. In France, we bought a pop-up beach tent and a football, again when we left we left that for the next guests. We are not attached to things like we (the parents) used to be. Before we made this transition, we had a four-bedroom farmhouse by the beach and we had SO MUCH 'stuff' we had two kids' rooms and a playroom full of stuff, I had two wardrobes with ten/fifteen years' worth of clothes in – clothes that didn't even fit anymore? Things I was just holding on to? I think it is definitely a process, both physically and mentally. When we started clearing out, I was emotional about it; I had attached so much emotion to all these things. Toys the kids had played with and outgrown clothes I wore for certain events in my life. Things bought for us by people we cared about. The process for me really cleared so much mental baggage I was holding onto that I was not even aware of. It left me feeling so free and empowered.

The kid's attitudes are abundance, they never feel lacking or without, and they are great at sharing. This makes us so happy, as many 'people' shared their fears and opinions about our kids' future issues, of not having 'stuff'. We have all we need and that is enough. I would highly recommend this lifestyle to others, maybe not as drastically as us we do not even have a home, but to get rid of the excess of 'stuff' people have and never use. When you are minimalists, it frees so much, space physically and mentally. As entrepreneurs, it cleared our minds and allowed us the mind freedom to create and grow into the leaders we needed to be to create our incredible businesses." — *Laura Helen (Forever Family Forever Free Blog)*

2.2 Common Misconceptions About Minimalism

When you tell someone that you're a "minimalist," they might immediately assume that you're a clean freak who goes ballistic over mess. But as mentioned earlier, it's way more than that. Now, let's expose all the common misconceptions about minimalism.

1. You Must Give Up Comfort And Convenience

Many people get intimidated by this lifestyle because they often think that it requires you to give up your belongings that give you your comfort on a daily basis. But you have to keep in mind that minimalism isn't about what you give up; instead, it's about what you keep. It's about keeping the things that carry value in your life and getting rid of the things that are holding you back from a more comfortable and pleasant life.

But for the sake of argument, then yes, okay… there are some minimalists who only have a couple of clothing items. But for most, the general rule is to focus on quality over quantity.

2. You Must Live Like a Monk

While most monks live following a minimalist lifestyle, it doesn't mean you have to be a monk and leave everything behind and live in a secluded place. While it's true that there are extreme minimalists who become monks, and vice versa, it's not necessary.

3. You Must Count Your Belongings

Although some minimalists would rather count the number of belongings they have, many minimalists don't which is perfectly fine. Many minimalists don't like to stick to a certain number because, for them, the number is not what's important – they prioritize on the fact that the things they own bring purpose or value to their like.

4. You Must Become Vegan and Live Zero Waste

Because minimalism is considered to be an alternative way of life, it's not surprising how it's still far from the mainstream. Similarly, living a sustainable lifestyle or being a minimalist is also considered an alternative lifestyle. This means that not because both lifestyles have something in common, it automatically means that one incorporates the other. The same way goes to living a zero waste lifestyle.

5. You Must Always Choose to Save Money

Another common misconception many people have about minimalism is that people who live by its principles are cheap. It's actually the other way around. As mentioned earlier, most minimalists make sure that they can get the very best of something, usually, disregarding the price tag. For example, if a minimalist person needs to buy a blender, he or she has to make sure that they can buy the best quality they can get. For a minimalist, it's better to buy something that is pricier as long as he can assure that he will be able to use it for years, instead of buying something that is very cheap but is expected to be disposed of after a few months of use. Rather than cheap people, it's more appropriate to label them as smart shoppers.

6. It Is all About Decluttering

This is no doubt the most common misconception about minimalism. For many people, a minimalist lifestyle is a synonym to decluttering. But the truth is that decluttering is simply a tool that is used to clear away the stuff that doesn't bring happiness or fulfillment into your life, in order for you to be able to focus better on things that do. While you can look at decluttering as a metaphor for ending something, decluttering on its own does not make you a minimalist as minimalism is a way of life, not a one-time action.

Minimalism lifestyle is not as intimidating as most people think it is. It doesn't restrict you to live a comfortable life. Instead, its goal is to give you a better life by highlighting things you should give more importance to.

Chapter 3

DEALING WITH CLUTTER IN LIFE

Clutter is a common challenge for many. This is known to keep you from being productive both from your work as well as personal life. Cluttered spaces are due to things not having their proper places, people shopping without a list or buying impulsively, being unable to decide whether or not you want to keep something because of its value.

These are usually surface reasons that cause clutter. However, the real reasons for clutter lie behind the surface and are connected to us physically and mentally. Regardless of how much paper or belongings you have, your clutter reflects who you are.

You are not able to clear the clutter by focusing on your belongings. How many times did you eliminate the clutter on your table or the pile of clothes next to your closet only to have it come back after a couple of days, making you feel like it's just impossible to get rid of the clutter? If this is something you experience on a regular basis, then it's possible that there's something else going on in the background that holds you back from letting go of it.

When you see beyond your physical clutter, you can then start to see its connection to your body and mind. So, how is your clutter connected to our physical body? Clutter can cause a lot of negative effects on the body including the following:

- A study shows that over-consumption of stuff is linked to over-consumption of food
- Aggravates allergies by promoting the buildup of dust mites, mold, dander, and other allergens
- Creates a haven for germs
- Delays you to do important tasks as it makes things hard to find
- Increases risk of injuries
- Its overwhelming presence drains your energy

Now let's take a look at how clutter affects one's mental perspective. Clutter is being accumulated in physical spaces once mental clutter starts to accumulate. The mental clutter is usually caused by stress, associated emotions, and small to big changes in life. When we are mentally cluttered, we find it hard to focus and often feeling mentally drained and heavy. The way we think usually represents how our physical environment looks like. Here are the ways clutter affects our mental health:

- × Abates your ability to make a decision
- × Escalates anxiety and stress
- × Inhibits you from living in the moment
- × Makes procrastination worse
- × Represses good things from getting into your life
- × Worsens symptoms of paruresis

By being aware of what goes on below the surface, it is going to be easier for you to do something about it. The plan of attack you will have will also affect your lifestyle changes on the whole. Once you clear up the clutter, it will affect different areas of your life. For example, once you get rid of the clutter in your room, you will be more motivated to do your task of the day and you will have one less thing to worry about which lowers the level of anxiety.

This also works the other way around. For example, when you are mentally and physically better, it gives you more motivation to declutter. So, before rolling your sleeves up and begin decluttering your space, take a look at it a little bit deeper and ask yourself, how does my physical and mental state affect my environment? Your mental and physical clutter presents the clutter in your environment. One of the best ways to getting rid of the clutter once and for all is determined by you.

3.1 How Decluttering Changes Your Life

It keeps the flow of energy

All things around us, including ourselves, are made of energy, and getting rid of clutter is effective in boosting your energy levels. Energy has to flow without restrictions, but when there's something blocking the way, it inhibits the flow of energy. Just try it. Do you have a room or space in your house that you wanted to be clean but due to certain circumstances, you can't find the time or the motivation to clean it? Just clean it and see how your energy changes. After the little makeover you give to your space, you will be rewarded with neatness, clarity, and of course, more space.

It saves you time

Is frantically running around looking for things you can't find a normal scenario for you? How many times has trying to look for your keys or wallet made you late for work? Having a lot of stuff means having a lot of things to manage. Similarly, having less stuff makes it much easier for you to manage things, which means whenever you need something it will always be easier to find.

It improves your mood

No matter how big or small the space you declutter or organize is, it will always boost your mood. A decluttered place feels like a safe place. This is beneficial for those who are suffering from anxiety and this is very obvious in people suffering from Obsessive Compulsive Disorder. For individuals who obsessively clean, organize, or count things, being in that "safe place" makes them calmer – even just temporarily. And while this is an extreme example, people with other clinical disorders may benefit from it also.

It gives you a chance to help those who are in need

By decluttering, you're not only helping yourself, but you can also help people who are less fortunate. Imagine doing something that is beneficial for you not only physically and mentally, but also spiritually! Some of the best things to donate are clothes, books, and toys.

It teaches children how to be appreciative

If you're a parent who wants to practice minimalism, note that there's nothing wrong with giving nice things to your kids, given you have financial means to do so. But you must also keep in mind that there should be a fine line between enough and too much. By letting your kids have too many things may teach them to be hoarders. You should be careful; otherwise, they may turn out to be spoiled. Instead of appreciating it when you give them a toy, feeling of expectation is likely what they may feel.

It encourages us to deal with emotional problems that may be triggering the clutter

As mentioned earlier, just like how physical clutter can generate emotional problems, clutter can also be due to an unaddressed emotional clutter. Whether it is a problem with your relationship, job, or habits, clutter can be a mask for life dissatisfaction. Once you make a move in getting rid of your clutter, these emotional problems have a chance to surface and there will be a space to address your unhappiness.

It opens up new opportunities

Imagine living your life without clutter. You will have more time to spend on things that truly matter to you. The way you approach life will change. Your self-esteem towards your relationship and social circle will improve. You can save more money and work towards your career growth. You will have more energy to spark creativity. By throwing away the unnecessary things in your life, more doors surely open for new and great opportunities – emotionally, physically, and spiritually.

Chapter 4

MINIMALISM IN DIFFERENT AREAS OF LIFE

After discovering the different aspects of this lifestyle, it didn't take long for me to realize how the benefits of minimalism are starting to affect each aspect of my life and not just my household.

Before this, I had a delusional description of minimalism. I, just like many people do, imagine people wearing capsule wardrobes with monochrome shades, a suitcase of clothes, or spectacularly simple-looking home with Scandinavian-inspired interiors. You have probably seen a lot of pictures dotted all over social media which make minimalism look like a lifestyle that only individuals with extreme self-discipline and a repugnance to shopping can be successful at.

At first glance, the minimalism lifestyle can be seen as superficial. The outwardly endless clear countertops and succulent plants in every corner of the room, and ever-diminishing closet seen on Instagram posts could be like and follower miners for some of those so-called influencers on social media. But there's a huge chance that they only embrace the idea of minimalism due to its aesthetic appeal.

This is not to say that there's something wrong with it. But this is to say that it could be deeper than that. Minimalism, for many who practices it, brings drastic changes to their life. The lifestyle is not only about how it can affect you visually or mentally, but it can also be about how it can affect every corner of your life.

4.1 Essential Relationship

First, let's talk about how minimalism can positively affect your relationships. The first way is that it encourages you to cut out unnecessary relationships, especially the toxic ones.

These relationships could be with a friend or a coworker that doesn't bring value to your life. Perhaps, they are rude to you or have a bad attitude. Perhaps, they have judged you or didn't show you respect. If there are people that are like this – may it be your romantic partner or relatives – minimalism can help you highlight the only things or people that you need in your life.

Minimalism can also help you realize that it's only you who control all the things you bring in to your life.

By adopting this mindset, you can learn how to live your life with purpose and commitment and help you accept the fact that some people that don't make you happy or make you unhappy should be let go once and for all.

Dating

By adopting minimalism to your dating life, you can start with zero and simply add on what's necessary to your relationship. This means giving him or her, the only things he or she needs – not anything unnecessary.

So, what am I talking about? These are the qualities that a relationship needs to make it stronger. These qualities include, but not limited to being:

- ❖ Supportive
- ❖ Accepting for who the person is
- ❖ Ambitious to attaining his goals
- ❖ Fun to be with

You can also seek these qualities when finding a person to be in a relationship with. This means removing the need to find someone who is 6-foot tall, has a fancy car or lives in a huge apartment.

If you choose to approach the dating scene the other way around, with a long list of "standards", you may end up accepting the wrong ones and overseeing the things that are more essential. "Yeah, he does work so hard and spends 80 hours at work, and has a luxury car."

This is not something that may likely benefit your life in the long run.

Applying minimalism on your dating approach may help you stay grounded. But of course, this is when you're ready to be serious and thinking about settling in already.

The truth is no one can tick off all the boxes on the list you might have put up. The only way you can check off all the boxes is if you list the small qualities that are deeper than material or superficial things.

There are many relationships that face fights and problems due to trivial things. Social media, unmet expectations, not saying things the right way, not reading the other person's mind, and even financial state can be trivial when you really dwell on the things that are more important in life. Minimalism helps us overlook those pointless things and just see the bigger picture.

Minimalism constantly reminds us of the positive sides of letting go. Just like how it restricts our attachments with certain objects in our lives, it also restricts us from routines and persons.

Stronger marriage

I just celebrated my sixth wedding anniversary, which also happens to be approximately my second year of following a minimalist lifestyle. The two are closely related in my life.

A couple of months before my wedding, I experience a mild panic attack. No, I didn't think about running away or ditching my then soon-to-be wife. The attack happened when a moment of clarity sunk in and I realized that I had to get my expenses under control or it could lead to some serious issue in my marriage. I sat on the computer and started listing my debts against my assets. I didn't get positive results. Right that very moment, I promised myself to only buy something if I really need them.

This was before I even heard anything about minimalism and I definitely hadn't applied the idea of it on anything that I am aware of. But then, there I was, telling myself over and over again to spend less money in order to have better married life. From then on, I have become increasingly devoted to following the lifestyle and up to this day, it has continued to be beneficial to my married life in a lot of ways.

Here are some ways minimalism has helped me and my spouse build and keep a stronger marriage:

Better control of our finances

There's no denying the divorce rate is still soaring, and it's also a known fact that financial problems are one of the main reasons for it. When the couple is open to each other when it comes to finances from the beginning of the relationship, there will be higher chances for them to have a successful, lasting relationship.

A relationship that follows minimalism may likely have a plan on how and where they spend their income, no matter how much it is. While there is no rule on how and where you spend the money, many minimalist couples try to spend less than what they make.

Honest communication

Being able to calmly and openly talk about money is not easy for many couples. But once they figure out how to do it, most aspects of the relationship become easier.

For me personally, I like thinking of my relationship with my wife as an open-source project. Every part of our relationship is transparent and anything can be discussed. From minimalism, I learned the importance of examining and acknowledging some of the less positive parts of myself and make a proper adjustment before they lead to serious problems that could ruin the relationship.

Less stressful and more affordable holidays

Instead of spending money on luxurious vacations, exchanging gifts, and having parties, minimalist couples would rather spend time together and making it special without the need to spend a lot of money. As a minimalist, you will see how easy it is to find a fun activity to celebrate these special occasions rather than exchanging gifts. This helps couples make the most of their time with each other without denting their savings. After all, that essence of celebrating an occasion is to commemorate the love you're sharing. On top of that, the overall stress of the holiday season can be reduced as you don't have to worry about the perfect vacation or the perfect gift to give to each other.

Better health

Minimalism teaches the concept of "garbage in, garbage out," which you can also apply to your relationship. Since the beginning of my marriage, my wife and I have made a shift from eating healthy home cooked meals to eating out. Our health, as well as overall spending, has improved radically because of it.

Support for passions and values

In the first year of our marriage, my wife and I have decided to leave our higher paying jobs in order to follow our career paths and goals that we are striving for, because we thought our old jobs were giving us unnecessary stress that brings toxicity into our life. We believed that we needed to go for something that is much more aligned with our passions.

Now, this is not to say that minimalism can make your marriage perfect or fix any problem you could have. However, I really believe that any couples can benefit from following the basic values of minimalism.

Another main reason for failed marriage is expectations. Many couples, especially the newly married ones, expect too much of a fairytale romance story.

We have been so molded by today's society into thinking that you will get a "happily ever after" once you're married, that our expectations are extremely high and extremely far from reality.

There have been a lot of studies comparing arranged marriages and traditional marriages, and the results are not what you'd expect. According to studies, the level of "happiness" continuously soaring over the years for arranged marriages, and on the other hand, going down on the years for traditional marriages.

So, what might be the reason behind this? It is said that it was because arranged marriages began with low expectations, that's why they were pleasingly surprised and happy when things surpassed those initial expectations.

As research on satisfaction judgments shows, when expectations are low, these expectations are easier to meet making the arranged wedding couple more satisfied. While in a free-choice marriage, on the other hand, high expectations usually develop throughout a lengthy dating period. This puts couples up for failure after going through the honeymoon period.

Again, when you have minimalist expectations, you begin with zero and just add what is truly important. Important expectations might include "he/she knows how to listen to me", "he/she comforts me when I feel down", "he/she supports my dreams and goals." and they DON'T include "he/she doesn't give me enough compliments", "he/she doesn't earn enough money to buy a nice car", or "he/she always doesn't as productive as I want them to be."

4.2 Parenting

For many years, my family has been following a focused simplicity lifestyle. We know how complicated life can be, and we choose not to be taken over by this complication. That's why we choose to live with a minimalist lifestyle. And one of its major benefits that truly affect our family life is how it changes how we approach parenting.

So, in what ways, you may ask... Here are the ways minimalism affects parenthood...

It encourages you to take parenting seriously

It has become a habit for me to read reading materials about minimalist living. This regular dose of inspiration constantly reminds me to focus and make the most of every moment I spend with my loved ones, especially my kids. After all, they're not going to be little kids forever.

As parents, every time we weigh the different activities and desires of our lives, our families are our top priority. Having a family is a huge responsibility and we must take it very seriously.

It keeps you from spoiling your kids

For many parents, they think that being a good parent means giving everything they could to make their kids happy. But you have to remember that there is a fine line between what your kids need and what your kids want.

It's important to learn when to say "no" to things that you know they wouldn't need in the long term. Similarly, there's nothing wrong about giving your kids something they want from time to time.

For me personally, I give my kids treats as rewards after doing something they worked hard for. For example, I promised my 6-year-old kid to buy him his own computer if he gets straight A's in his class. This is in the hope to make him realize that if he really wants something, he has to work hard for it.

It helps you choose your battles wisely

No, I didn't mean a huge heated conflict, when I said "battle". I'm talking about the problems that we, as parents, make a big deal of sometimes. I'm talking about those small differences we may have with our kids that turn into disagreements.

As parents, we tend to think that we always know better than our kids – we think that we always know what's best for them. From the food they eat, clothes they wear, the friends they hang out with, to what clubs or sports to join at school and what career path to take, we usually have suggestions and sometimes, we tend to push those suggestions upon them.

Minimalism teaches us that while there are always unlimited options, the capacity is always limited. We need to choose where we spend our time and energy. In our effort to guide our kids' transition from being dependent to independent, we must learn to let go and let them make decisions for themselves.

When it comes to arguments – which something that is inevitable – minimalists acknowledge that there are times to stand our ground and there are times when it's just not worth it.

Keep in mind that if everything is a big deal, then there is no big deal

When dealing with arguments or making decisions that will affect the happiness of our kids, you have to think of what's at stake – their trust on you. These arguments can be considered as clutter and can be extremely distracting and might even cost us more than they are worth.

You become more fixated in what you teach your kids

While we want to raise our kids with the truth, you must not let that deceive you. You have to keep in mind that all truth is not similarly important.

It's possible to follow accurate details all my life and not find purpose and happiness. There will be things in life that are definitely important for my children to learn more than anything else. I always see to it that I focus my guidance on those things and help them to stand out amid all the information that comes their way as they grow up.

This is my question for you: If your kids are only to remember a thing or two about what you teach them while they are still under your wings, what do you want them to be?

Once you answer the question, emphasize those things in all that you say and do. There are surely other ways that minimalism can improve your parenting, but for me, the points mentioned above are what stand most significant.

For parents like me, you know that being a parent is one of the best roles in the world. And, as parents, we have to do everything we can to eliminate the clutter that will hamper us from our very important responsibility.

4.3 Career Life

Have you fallen into the idea that in order to be productive, you should work day in, day out?

If yes, then this scenario is probably familiar to you…

You get up very early; go to your work to start grinding. When it's already lunchtime, you stay in your chair, eat there, while carrying on working. As your coworkers start to leave at the end of the day, you stay late while you try in vain to finish all of your tasks and projects.

Few months passed, you are excited by the thought that you are progressing in getting the goal you are trying to achieve. But as time passes by, you're starting to realize that you are not really as productive as you initially thought, and you are struggling to sustain the chaotic pace.

If you choose to live like this, it shouldn't come as surprise when you get too burnt out by the end of the year.

So, what's the connection between productivity and minimalism?

The first thing you need to know is that there's a little-known (but certain) connection between productivity and minimalism.

Here is how you can look at minimalism in connection with productivity: Delivering a task the simplest way possible.

This might mean planning how you can manage your emails proficiently or knowing how to prioritize important tasks over the ones that can be done later. It might even mean generating the ability to focus fully on the laid-out task. The goal of minimalism is to get the tasks done easier… and more productive!

An example is when you have streamlined the way you make and present reports, you might find that you could do this task way faster than the time that it took you before. It just requires some time management and creativity to find for you to make the task as easier and simpler.

If you find yourself constantly not having enough time to do other tasks aside from your work, you must take a step back, and start looking for ways to make your workload easier for you to deal with. Every task that you make simpler can help save you a lot of time.

In spite of what you might have been taught at school, productivity and minimalism are essentially connected.

8 ways minimalism can boost your work productivity

Now, let's take a look at some of the best ways to apply a minimalistic approach to your work.

✓ **Write a daily to-do list**

Start your working day (or any other day) by writing a to-do list. You can use a piece of paper or a smartphone app. It would only take a couple of minutes to create a list of all the things you'd like to do in the day ahead. And it is incredible how this simple activity could manifest your thoughts and help plan and carry out your day better.

✓ **Identify essential tasks**

When you have listed down all the tasks you need to put on your to-do list, scan through it. What are the ones you need to finish today? Can you identify them? In a lot of cases, the essential tasks should be finished first, and of course, listed down first. You can sort them out from the most important to the least important. Or some people like leaving exclamation mark (!) next to the item, so they can easily see identify the most critical ones.

✓ Learn to focus and defeat distractions

To be a successful minimalist, you must learn to develop laser focus. If you can't avoid distractions (such as loud conversations in an open-plan office), then by building powerful mental focus – distractions won't distract you anymore!

✓ Turn tasks into daily habits

Daily habits can be incredibly potent. They can break down complex tasks and turn them into bite-sized daily treats! For instance, you may work at a restaurant and need to clean the outside of the building every week. The cleaning might take you one hour to complete. Instead of this, you could build a daily routine of cleaning a part of the outside every day for 10 minutes. This will be easier and more enjoyable to complete than working a full hour on the task. It will also enable you to make it a habit – so you'll never have to motivate yourself to complete it.

✓ **Stretch time**

Stretching time is a skill that many people struggle with. But first, what does stretching time mean? Okay, so let's say that you are given two hours to create a slide show presentation. You begin the task, and if you are like many people, you will complete the tasks somewhere within the given two-hour mark. Now, imagine that rather than two hours, you were instructed to finish the task in one hour. Guess what – you can do it! This is what stretching time means. In order to save your time, try to assign yourself less time to finish your tasks.

✓ Be aware of the Pareto Principle

Have not heard of the Pareto Principle? No? But you probably know what 80/20 rule is, right? Well, they're the same thing! According to this principle, only 20% of our efforts will lead to 80% of our results. Now, look at it at the other way around… 80% of our efforts will lead to only 20% of our results! So, the trick here is to be fully aware of the 20% of actions that are generating most of the results. Be aware of these actions, concentrate on how you do them, and see how your productivity skyrockets.

✓ Take breaks on a regular basis

When you have a lot of things to do taking breaks from time to time is very tempting. But research has actually shown that those who are taking regular breaks from their work are actually more productive compared to those who don't. There are some science-backed reasons for getting regular breaks, which includes the fact that this is beneficial for maintaining our focus, help us remember important information and reevaluate our main goals. So, don't allow pressure to persuade you to keep working when you know to yourself that you need a break, which will trigger an instant boost to your productivity.

Begin adding these minimalist methods to your life right now. You will be surprised at how much productivity you'll get and more relaxed your mind would be by the end of the day.

4.4 Finances

We mentioned how minimalism can help us control finances on the earlier part of this chapter, but let's go a little bit deeper into this aspect of your life.

Again, minimalism can have a big positive effect on your finances in terms of saving money, getting out to debt, and building wealth. By applying a minimalistic approach can help you accomplish your financial goals easier and develop your attitude as you run through the process of building wealth. Let's talk about exactly how minimalism can help your finances below.

Minimalism can help you get clarity around your core values

As repeatedly mentioned above, minimalism has something to do with letting go of things that are not important in your life and focusing on things that really matter. The important things to you will normally play around your core values that when you identify, can help you with the process of eliminating things you don't need and embracing a more minimalistic approach to your life.

For example, if you love traveling, but you find yourself spending hours and hours on the internet browsing for items on sale to buy, which usually you don't really need, you can, instead, save that money to use on traveling, which something you know you really love.

On the other hands, if there are things that you really want to buy, try to not buy them right away. List them down and let a day or two to pass and ask yourself, "Do you I really need this item?" if you do, then go ahead and buy it, otherwise, just save your money for something else more important.

If you have not already, you can identify core values by asking yourself these two following question:

What are the experiences and things that really important to you?

Every time you look at your spending habits, does it align with your values?

Minimalism can mean buying fewer things, which of course, means spending less

A lot of people might not agree with this when it comes to this point as buying less doesn't necessarily mean spending less, but hear me out before rolling your eyes.

Most of the time, people purchase things because they're cheap and they think they're a great bargain. However, since they're very cheap, they're likely to end up purchasing more and more things they don't actually need and might even end up not liking. And rather than concentrating on their core values, it then becomes about focusing on how you can get a bargain rather than saving money.

So yes in a lot of instances, buying less means spending less which in turn means more money to pay off debt, to invest, and to save.

Minimalism allows you to focus on paying off your debt and saving

In keeping with the previous points, by buying less, you can have more money to spend on things that matter more to you, such as getting out of debt and saving money for your goals and for rainy days. It's going to be a win-win approach for minimalists – buying less means more clutter and potentially saving money

Minimalism brings contentment and peace of mind

Contentment and peace of mind are products of a minimalist's lifestyle. Having less clutter and avoiding compulsive buying can actually eradicate stress. And because you're just spending money on the things that really bring joy to your life, you'll have a great sense of satisfaction and happiness. You don't need to worry about keeping or maintaining or more importantly, paying for things you don't really need in the first place.

Deciding to take a minimalistic approach to life can be a major shift in lifestyle and is often a lengthy process. Even after several years, I continue to work on minimalism in my life, however, this approach to life is very fulfilling and totally worth it in my opinion.

Chapter 5

NEEDS & WANTS

Many are still confused with the difference between the things we need and the things we want. They crave for things they don't have and make themselves believe that they cannot simply live a good life without it, and often not satisfied until they lay their hands on what they want. When this mentality gets into a person to the extreme, it will usually cause destructive effects.

By letting this happen to us, we only have ourselves to blame. By putting our desires our first priority, things can be truly unpredictable. We are going to be required to live with our decisions and deal with them.

By living your life within your means does not necessarily mean you're always forgetting pleasure. It is simply about appreciating what life has already laid for you and accept the fact that having more doesn't always mean having it better.

Being in control over yourself can feel good, especially if it's something you have never done before. You will find that there are many other ways to feel satisfied without spending a lot of money and putting yourself in great debt. As cliché at it sounds... true happiness comes from the inside.

When you feel unhappy, chances are, that you have compared yourself to others, which leads to feeling inadequate. We tend to be jealous whenever we feel someone else is better at something that we want to be good at. However, when you stop comparing yourself to others, you will eventually get into the realization that your life could be truly fulfilling without always having what you want.

You don't have to fall victim to your urge to have everything you want. You can still be truly happy with what you already have. By searching from what's within you, we are able to find healthier ways to deal with your compulsions or anxiety.

So, you can take control if you really want to. Materials things should not have power over you and you can make a living simply with simple priority and high virtue.

Keep in mind that true happiness could simply be achieved once you start to accept yourself for what you are and forgive yourself for the mistakes you have committed. There's no need for you to make things complicated.

Knowing how to find the value in things you already have is a lesson anyone can take advantage of. If you cannot accept yourself, then don't expect to find true happiness and freedom from your insecurities.

5.1 What Is The Difference Between Things You Need & Things You Want

There is an enormous difference between the words "need" and "want".

Needs

Obviously, these are the things that a person needs to stay alive. The things we need include food, water, shelter, clothing and not much else in this category, really. These are the things we need to stay alive.

In economics, need is basically referred to as something that is very necessary for a human being to survive. When a person fails to meet his needs, it would likely lead to the start of disease and limitation to a person's full functionality and efficiently in society, and even death.

There are two types of needs: physical needs and subjective needs. Physical needs are ones that are tangible things or things that can be measured. This category includes the food we eat, the water we drink, the shelter we live in, and the air we breathe. On the other hand, subjective needs are the ones that are usually seen to maintain the health of our mentality. Examples of these are love from others, self-esteem, and approval.

Wants

A want is a thing a person desires, either in immediate time or later on in the future. Unlike the things we need, wants may differ from person to person. For example, you may want to have a new car, while another person wants to travel to another country.

Every person probably has his own list of things he wants, each with a different level of importance. Moreover, wants may also change throughout the period of time; unlike the things we need, which remain constant throughout our lifetime.

There is a fine line between these two and the gray area is when you badly desire to have a certain thing that it gets to the point that you're starting to think that it's something you need instead of want.

5.2 How To Identify The Thing You Need From Things You Want

It's easy to identify things that you need from the things you just want. Just ask yourself... Are you going to die without it? If yes, then it's a need. On the other hand, you will know if something is just something you want if you can literally live with it.

It's very obvious. We need shelter to live in. We need food to fill your stomach. Your neighbors would appreciate it if you looked at clothes to wear as a need. Your basic needs like these are non-negotiable, so you don't need to do get rid of them for the sake of minimalism and decluttering.

So, when do your basic needs turn into wants?

It is when you desire to have a bigger, grander house that is more than you need for your family, when you shop for too many food items that even usually expire before you consume them, when you buy a lot of clothes that you hardly ever wear.

When wants become problematic

Of course, there is room to indulge in things we want, but as minimalist, you must only indulge in things that truly add value to your life. It's so easy to add clutter to your life these days, with the convenience online shopping offers, along with the constant discounts given away by different stores, and family and friends who like to give us gifts that we might not necessarily choose on our own. You will end up getting unnecessary possessions, occupying spaces that you could have had used for things that truly add value to your life.

Fortunately, when you see the difference between your real needs and wants, you can easily arrange your belongings in a more minimalist fashion, in the detached and rationalized way. By being committed to decluttering in this way, you can potentially find more calmness within yourself.

While the process doesn't offer an overnight result, it surely is worth it. It takes time to look through all our possessions, but it is well worth doing because the end result could be beneficial to all areas of your life.

5.3 How To Distinguish The Differences Between The Two That Promote Minimalism

The straightforward answer to this question is very simple: The first step to minimalism lifestyle is to know the differences between these two. There are two major steps you need to do to get started in practicing this lifestyle.

Step 1: Spend at least a month or two getting rid of all the things you want. All of them – gone!

I know this is hard, but don't worry, once you're heading down the right path, and you have made all the necessary changes you need in your life, you are able to reintroduce your wants eventually, although, by the time that comes, you probably no longer want them anymore. Keep in mind that this is not to say that your wants are not important, in fact, they, in a way, add value to your life. However, they are not as important as the things we need.

Step 2: Once you've completely got rid of the things you want, the next thing for you to do is to reduce your needs by at least 50%. The more, the better.

Okay, you're probably thinking, "But I need a place to live! I have to eat! I need my clothes, and I love them!"

Okay, okay... you don't have to throw away everything: you don't have to move in a hut and eat just instant noodles. However, you can always significantly cut down your living expenses.

If you are renting, can you live in a smaller place to cut down your rent? Can you sell the gadgets you don't really need? Can you donate the clothes you haven't worn for a year or more? Can you lessen your expenses on food? Of course, you can!

While situations can be different from person to person, you can always reduce your expenses and live a lot more deliberately. This is the high price of pursuing a minimalist lifestyle. Unfortunately, a lot of people are not willing to pay the price. But then again, it is human nature for us to always want more. Especially today where consumerism blocks us from knowing how much is enough and too much.

But when you successfully detach yourself from the clutches of material things, you will worry less; and when you get rid of your worries, you can easily focus on more important things that give you happiness and satisfaction.

It doesn't mean you must go now and start throwing away every single thing you have, it's necessary for you to plan accordingly, and once you are ready, the right decision can easily be recognized.

All beautiful changes take time and need the right action taking. Changes are definitely scary, but they can really be necessary. And even though big changes usually take a simple move, they are not easy, but you know what they say: nothing worth doing is ever easy.

Chapter 6

Optimizing Life For Minimalism

In this chapter, we're going to talk about the step-by-step ways of becoming minimalist through the principles of decluttering.

I tried to find the exact definition of "declutter" and I definitely cannot find the results in any dictionary of English vocabulary. However, it's a word widely used by many people today.

I assume, though, it is a synonym for the word unclutter. According to Free Dictionary Online, declutter referred as "to simplify and/or eliminate mess, disorder, obstacles, etc."

On the other hand, the definition for the word, "clutter" can be easily found. In fact, it is found in any dictionary and it is defined as "a collection of things lying about in an untidy mass".

So, it just means that declutter is the antonym of clutter. It implies to arrange things, to put items in a place where they should be.

Now, let's look at the meaning of the word, "organize." This word implies, "to arrange into a structured whole; order".

So, every time we organize, we are putting them in the right order/place (decluttering) in a structure having an efficient and useful solution to keep those items (organizing).

Another term which complements the word declutter is the word "clean". It seems like every time you declutter a space, it gets cleaner; however, it doesn't always mean that the area is cleaned.

Clean, as you probably know, is actually the process of eliminating stain, dirt, dust, etc. Decluttering and cleaning go hand-in-hand -- you cannot perform one properly without the other.

Another word we usually hear when declutter is the center of the topic is the word "hoarding" – but what does it mean? In most dictionaries you'll find, hoarding would be referred to as "to amass and hide or store away; reserve in the mind for future use".

There are certainly different levels of hoarding. However, in general for this term, a hoarder is someone who is serious in collecting clutter thinking that those items are valuable and have great use in the future. This is the problem though, for people who are serious hoarders, everything has value to them. This results in the accumulation of things that sometimes can be out of control.

Now... how do these terms relate to minimalism? These are the keywords you initially need to understand to attain the real essence of minimalism and to learn how you can successfully apply it in every aspect of your life.

Now that you know the differences of these words, let's go ahead and talk about the ways in becoming a minimalist through the principle of decluttering.

6.1 A Simple Plan For Home Declutter

Having a good plan is one of the most essential steps of decluttering a home.

The reason behind this is generally psychological: By having a clear plan for attaining a goal, will give you more motivation. First of all, it helps you to have "the end in sight" and secondly, will give you easy-to-follow instructions, which is a lot easier than debating and thinking to yourself, "how should I clean the fridge today?" for example.

So, here's a simple plan to use on the mission of getting your home decluttered easily. By following your plans accordingly in a religious manner, you can easily complete the task in just a week, by putting in at least an hour a day. Sounds easy, right? Because it is.

First, you have to decide on the steps that you are going to implement for the task.

The following are the most important steps:

(Note: You can add or modify this list according to your preference or situation)

Step 1: Gather all the things that "bother" you and you no longer use.

Step 2: Categorize them into two groups - one group for the things you want to throw out and one group for the things you want to give away or donate.

Step 3: Have enough space for the things you don't want to throw away.

Step 4: Organize them into a storage space.

Easy, right? These are the basic steps for decluttering your house, and even if you only choose to follow these simple steps, you will already see a great improvement.

As you can probably notice, I did not divide the tasks by rooms/areas at home. This is because I believe that it could be quite frustrating to have a vague task like "declutter the living room". This could just lead to a low level of productivity

There should be specific tasks/steps to perform decluttering to each part of the house.

But going back to the point where I mentioned "things that bother you", you're probably wondering what this means exactly?

Okay, so look, the main objective of home declutter is to minimize the stress brought by clutter and to make your home a place where you can relax and feel good both mentally and physically.

So, if your kitchen, or even your bedroom is pretty cluttered, but it does not bother you and does not make you think that you need to do something about it, you can leave it alone for the meantime. You must focus first on the parts of the house that bothers you the most - the most problematic parts.

Once you find the parts of the house you want to take care of first, the next step is to estimate how much time every step would probably take. The estimation will depend on how busy you are and how big the area is. If doing the first step will require more or less an hour, setting it for one day will be enough. On the other hand, if it takes more than that, perhaps setting 2 days is good enough.

Generally, only the fourth step should take the longest and you can divide it into 3 to 4 days.

6.2 Decluttering Your Home

Home should be the most comfortable, safest place for us. But in order for it to bring us the relaxation we need and for it to nurture a positive effect, it has to be clean and well-organized. But by having piles of unwanted items all around the home, it can certainly hamper your chance to maximize the purpose of your home.

The main idea of living minimalistic sounds attractive to a lot of people. Many also aspire to do it, but it seems like it's easier said than done. But that's pretty understandable. But when you know how to do it right, you'll be on your way to a successfully minimalistic home. Here are some tips you can follow for decluttering any part of your house.

Pick the right time when you want to start decluttering

Don't start the process in one room when you know you won't have enough time to do every inch of the room. Maybe, it's best to pick a time when someone else can give you a hand.

For example, if you have one hour to spare to do some decluttering, and you know that decluttering the garage is not going to be realistic to be done in that sort of timeframe, you can move to another place in the house that would be more ideal. Perhaps the kitchen or the bathroom?

That is enough time to go through the cupboards or drawers and throw away the junk you no longer need. Doing so would be a great accomplishment.

Divide your home into different sections

As I keep mentioned earlier, don't do the entire home at once. Decluttering your home, especially if you're the only one to do it, is best done by taking one room at a time.

When you choose to declutter one cabinet in the kitchen, one cabinet in the bathroom, and all the cabinets in your closet at the same time, you will often find you will just lose steam quickly.

Whenever you have to declutter, you can always keep going back to that one room you're working on and throw more and more things until you are satisfied. This may sound like a lot of work, but finishing even just a room is super rewarding.

It's really important to make sure that you really focus while you're decluttering. Remove all the items out of that cabinet and go through each of them.

Make three separate piles

- ➢ The Keep Pile
- ➢ The Toss Pile
- ➢ The Donate Pile

When you're done putting the items on the right pile, dispose of the toss pile right away. Carry the donate pile and place it in the car. The next time you have to go with your car, you can drop off the pile at your local donation center.

So, what would this look like for each room? Let's talk about each room in the house.

- **Bedrooms**

As you browse around your master bedroom, do you see things that are not in the right places? Or things you no longer use and that could be moved to a better place, given away, or even thrown out? Below are some ideas you may want to consider:

- Is there a pile of magazines or books on top of the nightstand that you are planning to read, but can't find time to read?
- Are there accessories and jewelry that are unorganized or no longer used?
- Are there too many framed pictures all over the place?
- Is there rubbish under the bed?

When you start looking around, you will probably see a lot of things that need throwing out or moving into their proper place.

After clearing all the tabletop areas, now you have to start going through the shelves, drawers, and storage areas you have. Keep in mind that if you don't use it, it's probably better for it to go.

If you find clothes you no longer use, donate them. Some of the things you can donate also include shoes, bed sheets, blanket, and even curtains. Our goal is to minimize our stuff as much as possible. If you don't use it, there's no point of keeping it.

Now, it's time to do some cleaning. You've moved and organized a lot of items in your room. You've probably also noticed several areas that are filthy and dusty.

Clean and polish all the furniture. Decluttering involves cleaning and removing dust and dirt.

Now, let's look into what you want to keep and get the organization started. Perhaps, you can group items in your armoire better to keep them more organized and easier to find when you need them.

For things that you use on regular basis, place them where you can easily get them. No one wants to spend hours looking for keys in the morning.

Look around and see if you have to move anything else make any other changes to make the bedroom perfect.

- **Kid's Room**

Over the past couple of days, my wife and I have been working on decluttering the room of our toddlers. It is not easy. This is especially challenging because sometimes, they just can't help themselves but clutter even while you are cleaning. So, here is what we do to declutter them...

The toys are the first things I go through. And I get pretty ruthless when it comes to decluttering toys. All ill see is toys that are broken, have missing pieces or the ones I haven't seen played with for months so all are heading to the trash. It's unfortunate that many toys get put in a toss pile, but I still try to find ones that are ideal for donation.

Before organizing the kids closet, I go through their toys first. Of course, I first organize the ones that we are going to keep. The bigger toys go into the storage box we keep under the bed when not in use, while the smaller ones are on the shelves and smaller bins.

After organizing the toys, I go straight to the clothes. I do the same process once again, but this time, of course, with the clothes. The first time we decluttered, we had to let go of a lot of clothes. We sorted through the clothes and categorized them. Offseason clothes and clothes that would be passed down to the younger kids went into its specific box, while the others were prepared for donation.

You can repeat the same process for any room in your house. Declutter and organize one room and then move on to the next until the whole room is done.

- **Kitchen**

Having an organized workplace is going to help you to be efficient and effective in whatever you do. The same thing applies when you're working in a kitchen. If your things are placed all over the place, you might end up wasting a lot of your time looking for those kitchen utensils you need to prepare your meals. On the other hand, by having an organized and clean kitchen, your life is going to be a lot easier and you'll have a smoother cooking experience.

Here are some ways to organize the kitchen and declutter your kitchen area.

1. Rearrange your kitchen stuff. You can start with the drawers because they're very easy to organize and declutter. Think of the stuff in your kitchen that you'll be keeping or throwing away. What do you use regular, and what do you rarely use?

2. After organizing, start cleaning your kitchen item storage. Wipe and wash them down in order to remove dust and other unwanted particles in your utensils.

3. Put back all your kitchen tools after cleaning the storage. Yet, you need to consider the flow of your movements within the kitchen. Think of how you prepare and cook your food. By doing this, you'll have an idea where you can place the important kitchen tools and those that are hardly used. Put all your pans and pots organized properly and your spices and condiments in the pantry.

4. Have just enough storage boxes. If you think you don't have enough storage space, then maybe you should try and make some. By doing this, your kitchen items are only going to be contained in one place. You could also use a separator so you can easily differentiate the knives from your other cutleries.

Furthermore, big appliances that are in your kitchen such as the refrigerator must be far from the door. This is an important thing to consider when you are looking to organize all your things.

In order to organize the kitchen and declutter kitchen things can be very easy regardless of how big the kitchen is. You should try and think what will make you more effective and efficient in your chores.

- **Bathroom**

Decluttering your bathroom can be one of the bigger challenges to organizing. While it's usually the smallest part of the house, we can usually find a lot of things in it. Fortunately, there are a lot of easy organizing techniques and products that can help you keep your bathroom looking decluttered and organized.

With a little creativity, you can successfully declutter your bathroom in no time.

Take stuff out of your bathroom, what are the things that you really need and don't need. Carry a garbage bag along with cleaning supplies

Go through those drawers. Throw out the old makeup if it's not being used anymore! You can move those items you store on top into a drawer. Your bathroom is going to be less cluttered. Using drawer organizers helps keep your bathroom drawers in order and don't forget to put those items you frequently use on top.

Is your body wash, shampoo, and conditioner sitting on the floor of your shower or on the handrail of the door? Has your shower floor turned into a blend of bottles? Are you tired of bending down to pick up what you need? You can also find different kinds of affordable and stylish shower caddies available today that will not only declutter and organize your shower but will also add aesthetics to your bathroom.

You can literally make the cabinets in your bathroom an organized storage area, neat and decluttered. First of all, you need to organize and purge! Get rid of that old shampoo that you bought and did not like. The same goes for anything that you have not used. I know that a lot of the time we buy things that we don't like but hate the idea of throwing them away. Now is the time to throw it away and organize your bathroom cabinets.

General Guidelines

- Check the drugs/medications that are past the expiration dates, throw out the expired ones.
- Establish a ruthless mindset
- Establish another storage area for rarely used items so they don't clutter your bathroom but are still easily reached
- Keep massively sized products bought at warehouse stores elsewhere
- Makeup also expires!
- Put an old sheet or beach blanket on the floor to use as a temporary staging area.
- Use your storage space only for items you are still using and use regularly
- **Living Room**

A lot of people are reluctant to consider organizing their living room. They think that because the living room is for living in, it's natural for this part of this house to accumulate clutter. But this shouldn't be different from other parts of the house when it comes to decluttering – a better living room is better to live in.

First of all, consider every activity that takes place in the living room and then decide if those activities are best done in this part of the house. Is it the best place to teach your kids their assignment? If you would rather make a comfy corner for your kids to study, then do that. Otherwise, consider defining a special corner for your kids when you need to help them study.

Try to work systematically, one category at a time, pull all things out of each space and group items as one. Make decisions on what you are going to do with those items based on the answer to the questions, "When was the last time I used this?" "Does it serve its purpose?" "Can't I live without it?"

Always be honest with yourself and cut back your items; if you are being honest, it is going to be easier to make decisions. Have specific boxes that you can label 'charity', 'sale', and 'keep'. If you have not decluttered this area for a long time, remember that what you loved and used before, might be something that you no longer need now. When you have decluttered every category and put everything on where they should be, moving around the living room would be a lot easier and more comfortable.

Top tips for decluttering the living room

- Take your time to evaluate what is working and what is not working in the space.
- Only keep items that you love and currently use.
- Ask family members whether or not they want to keep the items.
- Use the chance to clean as you go.

- **Garage**

Believe it or not, most people choose to leave their vehicles out on the driveway all the time. Normally, this happens because there is no room left in the garage to actually park their car, as they are just rammed with junk. If you are having the same dilemma, you may not want to miss this one.

You can start your garage decluttering process by looking through every item in the garage, one by one. Consider how long the item has been stored in the garage. If it's something you haven't used for more than three years, then maybe it's time for it to go.

One of the most common items people seem to love keeping are cans of paint. This is something that just has to go. It's possible as well that they are partly dried up already anyway.

There are a lot of things that make their way into the garage. Sports equipment is another culprit that gets 'permanently' stuck in the garage. Stop keeping any sporting items that are already broken. It's not a good idea to play tennis using a broken racket.

Of course, auto parts are always found in the garage. If you no longer have the vehicle that the parts belong to, it's time for you to throw them away. And of course, if they are broken just dispose of them right away. The next thing to evaluate is ladders. Unless they are in good condition, safe, and sturdy enough to be used, there shouldn't be a place for them in your garage.

Go through everything and even evaluate your tools. Think about how often you use each item, dispose of any items that you never use. If it's broken and cannot be fixed then, of course, throw it away.

Organize what's left

When you're already done and all of the clutter is out, it is time to start organizing. First, see how much space your vehicles will take up and then use what's left by placing items in the spaces based on their types and uses:

Regularly Used: Keep items that you use on regular basis. This includes rugs, shopping bags, and pet leashes within easy reach – maybe on hooks by the door.

Bigger Items: Use the two back corners of the garage to keep bulkier items like a lawn mower or snow thrower.

Hardly Used: Place items you rarely use like seasonal decorations or snow tires, on higher shelves of sturdy shelving units or you may want to consider installing a ceiling storage system. Just see to it that these new storages are not blocking the door.

Tools and Bicycles: Tools like rakes and shovels and bicycles are best stored by hanging on the wall.

Note: If you are using cardboard boxes as your storage containers, you might want to consider investing in some plastic bins that are going to keep insects, molds, and rats from taking up residence in your house.

Keep it tidy

When you're finally done with everything, you will have a cleaner garage that's organized nicely. The next step is to make efforts in maintaining your garage in that state by doing the following.

- ✓ Keep floor space as free as possible.
- ✓ Spray for pests every now and then to keep insects at bay.
- ✓ Sweep and scrub down the floors on a regular basis to remove dirt.
- ✓ And the most important step of all: Repeat the process at least every two months.

Keep only the things you absolutely love.

There is no point in keeping things just because. Really, keep only the things that you really love! I think there's nothing wrong with keeping an item that reminds you of your childhood – but don't keep all of them!

I know this is something that is difficult for many people. It can be difficult for some to give up the sweater their grandma gave them when they were little or for parents, their kids' clothes. But always remember that those are only material things and memories are forever and something can be built over and over again.

You might have items you don't really want to keep around, but you still actually need to keep. For example, certain cleaning supplies. In this case, I'd suggest only keeping just one of each needed item. Having something like 5 different window cleaners is just not necessary. Also try to pare down cleaning rags and other smaller miscellaneous items. Keep it simple!

Now that you've organized your space, maintaining it should be the next thing you need to worry about. You probably don't want to hear this, but decluttering is a process. Especially if you are decluttering a house.

The good thing is, once you have totally decluttered your house, maintaining it will not be as difficult.

As more or new things come into your house, take out the stuff you have no longer value for. Always think of the reasons why you wanted to live a simpler life and declutter, to begin with. Don't go back to how it was even before you get started.

Creating a housekeeping routine is an effective way of maintaining your home. My wife and I switch morning routines that keep our home clean and decluttered.

6.3 Decluttering Your Material Possessions

Are You Possessed by Your Possessions?

This is the first question you must answer if you are thinking about decluttering. So, what can you do for your possessions to possess you?

Now that I discovered the benefits of decluttering, clutter has become something that truly gets to my nerves. You can call me a neat freak.

After letting go of most of my possessions, I immediately reap the benefits it offered to me and my family. On top of the mental benefit it offers, I also enjoy the fact that I can now easily locate everything I needed.

Throughout the process of decluttering our home from possessions that don't add value to our lives, there are several things I and my family learned...

1. It helps in letting go of the past to make more room for the future

The whole decluttering experience will make you realize that that most of the things you are holding on to have already served their purpose in your life and at some point, you have to let go. It's very difficult to move ahead in life if you keep clinging to the past. Letting go of the sentimental items can be very hard. Seeing the old greeting cards, photos, and mementos lets you close chapters of your life that ended but you still keep holding on to.

It helps you free up mental energy for future undertakings and relationships. One of the most important things you'll realize throughout the process is that all items you dispose of or donate to charity already served their purpose. They might have given you a lot of joy or taught you a great lesson. By understanding this, you are freeing your mind for future experiences and development.

2. It teaches you to be grateful for what you already have

Again, there's nothing wrong with material things and in fact, I still have a lot of things that I find hard to let go of. However, I never let them become a priority to the point that they drag me off my track. For me, throwing away material possessions that are not being used, help free your mind from unimportant things and help you focus on things that are truly important, this on top of helping you grow as a person, improving your relationships, and helping others along the way. By surrounding yourself with only things you love, it helps you realize that there's no point of going nuts over a new gadget or garment. And more importantly, it helps you see the concept of quality over quantity.

3. It improves your sense of focus

When there is a pile of rubbish on my desk, I always find myself struggling to finish things I'm working on. But the moment I clear up my desk and put everything in their right places, working becomes easier. From a neurological standpoint, this completely makes a lot of sense.

Whether it is your office desk or bedroom, the mess in your surroundings can lead to a negative effect on your capability to focus and process the train of thoughts. That is exactly what neuroscientists at Princeton University discovered when they looked at task performance individuals in an organized versus disorganized environment. The final conclusion of the study showed that the physical clutter you have in your surroundings contends your attention, these results in lower levels of performance and higher levels of stress.

Clutter essentially triggers the brain to multitask. So, getting rid of it will help transform you into a concentrating machine.

Effective ways to get rid of unnecessary possessions

- **Tear down the museum**

I used to be fearless in my youth. I made a lot of friendships and made a history for myself that seemed worth to remember. So, I held on to all the trinkets from my past. Going forward to the future, I was rewarded with a lot of items that I did not have any room for in the present. I wanted to invite people over the house and even throw a party, but I couldn't even figure out where to put them all. So, what I did was, I took pictures of the items that were important to me, but I was still ready to let go. They are always going to be parts of my past, but they can't be with me, physically, forever.

- **Evaluate real value**

Most of the items I owned that have value to me were computer equipment. Every time I looked at it all, I would just see dollar signs. But then, looking at their economic perception, it was just a delusion. I was giving importance to those old computers based on the money I spent on them instead of their current market value: almost nothing. During decluttering, I sold many of my used electronics and sold them for $70.

- **Not everything is worth the fix**

Most of the broken things that piled up in my garage are gym shoes. I didn't throw them away because I was convinced that I will be able to get them fixed eventually. My wife held the shoes up in front of me, one by one, and asked a couple of questions: "If you saw a pair of these shoes in a store today, do you think you're going to buy them?" and "How much are you willing to pay for them if you're willing to buy them?" I admitted that I wouldn't buy those shoes again.

- **Inform your loved ones**

I'm a part of a minimalist group on Facebook, where minimalist people share their minimalist lifestyle-related thoughts and questions. One of the "dilemmas" members are experiencing is the number of gifts they get on special occasions. You see, this is something that shouldn't be a problem for many, in fact, it's a good thing. But for someone who tries to live in a minimalist lifestyle, this is something that can be a trigger for them for accumulating more and more stuff again. The solution to this is simple. Let them know about your lifestyle and tell them what you'd rather get. This could be a specific item that you like or even money.

- **Just admit that you don't like it**

As I organized my stuff, I slowly become aware of the fact that I did not even want to keep it all. There were things that I didn't really like but I didn't particularly hate either – and kept with them out of pure apathy. These are the easiest things to let go. It has only taken me a little motivation to pack up a couple of boxes and give them away to those who need them more.

- **Know what you really need**

Usually, what we need is just related to the thing we have. For example, I had an oven toaster, but I decided to let it go because I had a small toaster that is enough to toast my loaves. I also loved reading and my books were dear to me, but I made a decision of rehoming them.

- **Let go of the guilt**

When my grandpa passed away, I inherited his collection of 30 rusty knives, 5 toolboxes, and a copper watch he loved to wear. For many years, I kept them all. Eventually, I realized that if my grandpa was alive, he would probably replace the knives and the toolboxes. I disposed of them, but I kept the watch and still wear it from time to time.

- **Accept that "one day" may not even come**

Most people hoard stuff because they think that a time will come they will have to use them. My wife kept the wedding dress she wore 7 years ago. She didn't want to throw it away. But it was just taking too much room in our closet. Also, unless we are planning to remarry or wait for our 5-year-old daughter to get married and inherit it, no one is really going to use it.

6.4 Decluttering Your Gadgets

There is no denying that technology can truly make life easier and more entertaining. It also helps us connect with our loved ones from anywhere in the world at any time. But between necessities such as computers, smartphones, cameras, as well as old favorites such as the CD or cassette tapes collection, you have collected throughout the decades, you surely have a big a pile of clutter from this.

You might feel a little overwhelmed just thinking about organizing everything from chargers to cables to cassette tapes to computer accessories. However, when you do it, you will enjoy how your home becomes a much safer and more comfortable place, and you no longer need to waste time looking for misplaced headphones and memory cards.

Why it's important to organize your tech

First of all, it can help you realize why you are actually doing the process of decluttering in the first place. Safety is one of the main reasons; neglected cables can be a fire hazard, and cords or gadgets left underfoot can lead to tripping. Another reason is cleanliness; it's harder to vacuum, dust, or wipe down a cluttered area, so getting rid of that barrier makes cleaning a lot easier and so much more likely to get done.

Another motivator is aesthetics, of course. Large unused appliances, ugly wires, and remote controls lying all over the place can make even a well-organized room look untidy.

Lastly, technology must make your life easier, not more difficult. If searching for the right charger or adapter, or just plain use of any of your devices gives you stress, that is all the more reason for you to declutter.

Tech clutter hotspots

Every home has particular areas that are easily overtaken by technology and its associated clutter. And while these hotspots will vary from household to household, the most common clutter culprits are the following.

Around outlets

There is always a place where all the cables snake along the floor — or for wall-mounted TVs, skid down the wall. Some of the most effective ways to deal with this include hooks and clips that stick to your desk or walls, clamping cords down in better order; slim tubes that suit over cords and can be set up to the wall or floor then painted over, almost blending the cables into the wall; and boxes that fit over power strips, concealing the unappealing gathering of plugs. A lot of big hardware stores and websites offer an apparently endless collection of products to help organize cables and cords. By searching for "cord/cable organizer" online, you will have a lot of products to choose from and definitely find the one that is perfect for your needs.

Home offices or other designated work areas

Computers, printers, and other office supplies are usually found here. And because it's a place where you spend endless hours to work, you will want to make sure that it is a comfortable place. In order to clean up your workspace, the first thing you need to do is to get rid of any tech you no longer use, such as old laptops and broken spare parts. After that, you must determine how often you use all the things that are left. The things that you use all the time, such as the laptop can always be left on your desk but try to move the ones you rarely use like the scanner maybe. Put them on a shelf and just get them down when needed. When you need to upgrade or replace an old device, you may want to choose devices that perform multiple tasks. For example, instead of buying different devices for printing, scanning, photocopying, find a single device that is capable of doing all these three things.

Entertainment areas

These are usually found in the living room and bedroom areas. In order to clean up these areas, you can focus on clearing surfaces by baskets or boxes where you can put all your small tech stuff when you're not using them. Once putting back the remotes to the basket has become a habit, they will no longer clutter up the place. This means no more fishing for the remote under in the sides of the couch!

That spot near the door where items usually accumulate

This could be a kitchen counter, console table, or the first piece of furniture you see as soon as you enter the door, where you leave your phone, together with your keys and glasses. You don't have to fight the urge and convenience of putting your things here but adapt with your habits and the layout of the space and out a tray or basket in this clutter zone. This will help you keep small items from cluttering up the area and also prevent them from strangely wandering off.

Organizing your collections

The abundance of new technology — mixed with ever-growing shopping opportunities —makes it easier than ever to accrue gadgets, whether your weakness is for new camera lenses or audio equipment. And even though music lives in the cloud today, and watching movies can be done online, many people still don't want to give up their records, DVDs, VHS tapes, cassette tapes, and other collections you have built around earlier times of technology.

Collections have made a lot of people happy — but that changes when you already have to organize them. As with any decluttering project, the first step is to be truly honest with yourself and of course, get rid of the ones you no longer use. You can bring old CDs to a state or local government recycling center, if that's available in your area, or send them by mail to an organization such as the CD Recycling Center of America. You may also want to send them along with the CDs of old installation software and user manuals you have no use for anymore.

Next, manage the items that you hardly use, like old home movies you haven't watched in decades but impossible to let go. You can store these collections out of sight and out of your way in a basement, or storage unit. Pick containers that can protect your items from mold and water damage, pack them properly, and put a clear label on them. You must be aware that extreme changes in humidity or temperature can damage electronic gadgets.

Now it's time to arrange everything you want to keep easily accessible. The easiest storage options are attractive boxes or open shelving. Measure the size of your collection carefully before you buy any new storage accessories or furniture; Take a bookshelf that is too big or a cabinet that is too small and not just will you have tech clutter, but furniture clutter too.

If you're thinking about where to put your collection, choose the general organizing guidelines of keeping items close to where they will be used, which means, remote controls should be closed to TV and audio system.

Sorting out the small things

A great deal of tech clutter is due to the accumulation of small add-ons and accessories: power strips and cables, headphones and thumb drives, chargers and batteries, memory cards, as well as their little plastic sleeves, those small foam earbud covers, and so forth.

The moment you have removed anything you know you will never need again, the easiest way to arrange small tech items that will keep them all in a proper place: a cupboard, a shelf, a box, or anything as long as it works in your home. By doing that, you would not have to race from the hall closet to the office to the basement whenever you need to use an extension cord or an SD card.

However, a different method may work better for your specific situations. For example, if you always travel, you may want to keep travel-related gadgets items – such as external chargers and adapters – in a small pouch in your luggage. Or, you might want to keep the technology you use for work or a specific hobby in the rooms where you only use them and keep other household tech items in a different place.

As a rule of thumb, you should work with your own lifestyle and personal preferences. If you always instinctively check your kitchen drawer every time you need extra batteries, then put them there. If your house has an area that is specifically good for storage, make good use of it. When you declutter and organize, keeping it up should feel easy and natural. If you're having trouble, you are probably trying to defy your instincts or the arrangement of your space.

And again, labeling everything is a game changer; this could save you a lot of time whenever you have to identify which cable goes with which phone and other devices. You can use a label maker for an even look, or just get tape and a marker. Using colored tape is always a good idea to identify amongst a sea of black and white cords. In order to keep cords from getting untidy, wind them all and secure it using a bread wire tie, cable tie, rubber band, or Velcro strip before putting it back to the drawer or box.

Getting rid of unwanted tech

If you have a stack of unused laptops, cameras, phones, and other various gadgets anywhere in your home, you're not the only one. If you are holding on to them for a reason that you are no sure of, ask the product manufacturer or your local government in order to see if they have a recycling program. A lot of companies like Staples, Best Buy, and Apple offer electronics recycling services. You can also donate old computers and other items to charitable organizations, or make some money by donating them.

A lot of electronics are made with hazardous materials and shouldn't be just thrown in the trash; your city or county must give instructions on how to safely throw away these items in your area. And ensure that your personal information is removed and all hard drives are properly backed up, and carefully overwritten or erased.

As mentioned already, you are able to recycle CDs of the installation software and user manuals you don't have a use for anymore. You could probably declutter your paper user manuals as well; see to it that the information is found online, and then recycle all those little booklets and empty some space in your household files.

Decluttering is part of life, and like technology, it can inspire you to keep going and organizing additional parts of your home.

Technology is continually evolving, which means a lot of households are always acquiring new gadgets as older devices become out-dated.

While we are usually desperate to own the latest gadgets in the market, we are less eager to clear out what we currently have. This mainly boils down to not having an idea on what to do with old smartphones, laptops, audio players, and so on. On top of that, worry over getting rid of something that is important – a cord we are abruptly going to need, for instance, or confidential data.

However, nobody has space for old devices and cords to be piling up in their homes; so, here are some effective tips to declutter your gadgets:

6. 5 Decluttering Your Schedule

Reducing the number of your possessions is essential to embracing a minimalism lifestyle. However, what is equally important is decluttering your schedule and limiting what you put on your calendar.

With today's technology, housework, job meetings, meal prep, and dealing with family needs has become much more efficient. Technology surely has the capability to save us a lot of time. But why is that it seems like we are much busier than those who lived decades ago?

The reason for this is partly because it is something we want.

Today, having a busy schedule has become the main indicator of high status. We boast about how full our calendar is and how many individuals are competing for our time. We tend to think that this shows how important we are.

We live busy lives – may it be by choice or circumstance. Nonetheless, it's a reality of the world we live in today.

Because of this, there are a lot of people who are hoping to minimize their schedule but cannot seem to find the margin to do so. In this part of the book we are going to look into this further.

But first of all, how is decluttering your schedule beneficial? While decluttering a schedule is obviously a great way to repel the temptation of procrastination, there are other ways it benefits a person in a way that it supports the minimalism lifestyle.

- **Create more free time**

This may sound a bit backward because a lot of people think they are procrastinating when they choose to do nothing instead of spending their time working. However, if you come to think of it, it's only considered procrastinating if you have got assignments to do but choose not to do them. By decluttering your schedule, you will be able to make time in your day when you can just relax and do anything you want – you will know how to get things done by a specified time. By doing this, you will not be able to waste your free time worrying about what you must be doing for the time being.

- **You know when you're being unproductive**

Sometimes, it's not easy to acknowledge whether we are using our time wisely or not. For example, those who work online don't have bosses to tell them what to do or watch over you if you are doing your work right. If you have to follow a schedule and follow it, you will know what to do and what you should avoid. If you cannot finish things within a schedule, you can pinpoint what distracted you and so you can eliminate this next time around.

- **You can have peace of mind**

Do you constantly say, "There are not enough hours in the day"? You may think you have lots of things to do but not have enough time to get them all done. But by decluttering your schedule, you will have the peace of mind knowing that your tasks will get done without needing to lose sleep and forgetting to do other things.

- **You can set your goals accordingly**

One of the best things about schedules is that they can also be used as you goals. It's not hard to be thrown off-course in terms of achieving something. You can assign time to tasks that are going to help you to attain a long-term goal, such as being able to lift 300 lbs weight at the gym by the end of the year, as well as short-term goals, like finishing work's assignment by the end of the day.

- **Learn how to set a deadline**

When you are working on one thing, it's so easy to forget other tasks that are equally important. No one wants to pull all-nighters studying and working only to remember that you forgot to finish something that is due the next day. You are can highlight your deadlines on your schedule in order for you to have a clear vision of how much you have to accomplish before they arrive. Then, you can make a decision whether to do your projects all at the same time, or for a short period of time.

- **You don't double-book**

So, someone asked you to go out on a Friday night, and you agreed. But then you realize too that you have got something else important to do at that time. You don't want that person to drive all the way to meet you while you ditch the plan, however, you can't also ditch that important thing you need to do. You can avoid disasters like this by always being aware of what you need to do and when.

- **Being more productive**

There is nothing that improves productivity better than a schedule. When you are looking at all the things you have to accomplish in the following days, weeks, months, or years, you are bound to be more efficient as you know you don't want to be stuck with everything last minute. You can jump from task-to-task rather than thinking you have more free time than you actually have. In the end, you will probably see that you have accomplished a lot so that you can now relax have more time to relax.

Now that you know the benefits of decluttering your schedule, how can you experience these benefits? Here are effective ways to declutter your busy schedule.

1. Wake up early or stay up late

In a perfect world, you can choose whenever you want to be productive. Sit down on your desk, start working while waiting for the day to end. Unfortunately, being productive is not as simple as just plugging in for humans—we experience a kind of energy and creativity at a certain period of the day.

So, when is the right time for you to work? Some of us are naturally born as either an early bird or a night owl. According to research, we cannot choose to be a night owl or a morning bird, because our biological clock, or chronotype, is mostly genetic.

Now, only about 15% of us are real early birds, and 20% are natural night owls, while the rest of us are in-between. Now, you're the only one to decide what you truly are. Find out what you are and choose what time of the day, or night, you are more productive and then set your schedule depending based on when you are productive.

2. Turn off the television/wi-fi

According to statistics regarding our screen time, we spend an average of about 10 hours a day in front of the TV or computer. Aim to reclaim your control over your life and home by reducing your time in front of your electronics. Ideally, you may want to spend only 45 minutes a day. I know this could be a drastic change for many, but don't worry because this does not have to be a permanent change if you find it difficult, but it wouldn't hurt to try. So, for a period of time, it is able to give you the extra time you need to declutter your home during a busy schedule.

3. Clarify your priorities

Clarifying your priorities is another important step to decluttering your schedule. To me, my priorities include my family, job, time with nature, spare time for reading, going out, etc. Every time I look at my schedule, it was full of tasks like happy hour, social events, and weekends are full of housework. When I decided to make a change, I stopped committing to most of those events and suddenly, I had free time to do constructive things like going for overnight camping or visiting my parents.

4. Reignite your passions

When I had the free time I always wanted, I had to find out what I really loved and wanted to spend most of my time doing. I completely got rid of the things that were holding me back from doing what I loved. After decades of being super busy with school, work, social life, and family, I didn't know what my true passions were. It was not until I had the free time to try new things that I discovered this (I got into painting, started a blog, and started reading more again) soon I found out what I truly loved. I am into art. I love to read and write. Now that I have decluttered my schedule, I can easily do these things, whenever I want to.

5. Look for something deeper

The thought of traveling the world was very exciting to me in the beginning. When I actually started doing it,

I felt like it was much more rewarding when I could actually share my experiences. I started writing about what I had learned on my blog, and how minimalism changed my life and led me to follow my goals that I'd pushed so far away for a long time. Today, I'm living my life happy and satisfied, knowing that I always do something that will not only enhance my life as well as the others.

6. Learn how to say no

It seems like 24 hours a day is not enough to do what we want and need to do. We have to acknowledge that even though there are a lot of things we can do, we don't have to do them all at the same time. Saying no to the things that are not a priority can be hard at first, but it's possible and also fulfilling. Eventually, I made a massive goal of going on a big travel trip with my family, which made my priorities much clearer and made it much easier to say no to happy hour or social events that did not help me acquire to this goal.

Saying "yes" is not always saying yes

Saying "yes" to all things actually means that you have time for nothing. You cannot possibly say yes to everything, or else there wouldn't be enough time for you to do all the things that are important. I mean, how could you possibly get all your work don, meet everyone you have to meet up with all at the same time? Your days will be so hectic, you would not be able to rest, and more so, you would not be able to do the things that are more important.

Saying yes doesn't necessarily mean you're saying yes – it just means you can't manage your time and set your priorities right and make some serious commitments.

Take this approach: if you find it hard to say "YES!!!" in an enthusiastic way, then, it probably means no. BUT other people don't know that! So, you must learn how to be straightforward.

Say no to more, and make your life simpler.

Ask questions before filling up your calendar

Every time you look at your calendar, don't look for tasks you can remove in place of another. Instead, choose what things are important enough to stay. Ask yourself these important questions:

Is this thing important for me enough to improve my life?

- Is this the most important thing I should do at this specific moment?
- Does this get me closer to my priorities/goals?
- Is there something more productive that I need to be doing?

Decline requests for your time

Separate your decision from your relationship. Just because you say no to something doesn't mean the person who asks you the question isn't important to you.

Have present boundaries. This may just mean that Saturdays are meant to be spent with family or using your Friday night to finish some of your assignments. Be firm with your boundaries. Yes, it might not be easy, but in the end, it'll do you a lot better and also teach you how to value people's time.

Keep in mind that when you are focused, you will be able to accomplish more things. There are times when we are asked to get involved in something, we say yes even though we are busy because we think that we can still "squeeze" it in. But remember you want to try and declutter your schedule, not fill it up. It's important to limit what you allow on your calendar, and only put in things that really matter.

How to say "no" so that you won't offend people?

"I appreciate it for asking me, but unfortunately, I won't be able to go."

"I'm sorry, but I'm occupied during that time. I'll be free on Wednesday next week, though."

"I'm honored that you would like my help, but I'm not in a situation to give it the time it deserves."

"I'm sorry, but I'm busy doing something else at that time and it's very important."

"Thank you for inviting me! However, I already have plans with my family, so I will have to pass on that one, sorry."

You can always say "no" in a nice way without offending the other person.

People can easily understand "yes" and "no", but saying "maybe", that's something you should avoid!

Saying maybe can lead to a big disappointment on their side. A vague question is no better than ditching them after saying yes. If you are not sure, ask them for more time to think about it. Tell them you will get back to them after a day or two to see whether you can make it or not.

If you are aware that you have previous engagements and you just can't make it, just let them know right away. It isn't fair to the person who is waiting for you to say yes who will only be disappointed when you don't answer.

Chapter 7

A Life Of Abundance

Last year, I went on a trip with my wife to Cambodia. As you know, this country is a developing nation. But you know what amazed me about this country? Their people! You see, most locals I met during my stay sit on the poverty line, and even though they have few possessions, they were the most joyful people I've ever met.

The little kids I had met were the happiest and most appreciative children I have ever encountered. And for many of them, instead of playing with toys, they were forced to work at an early age in order to survive. This is something you will hardly see in western culture.

Seeing the joy in their eyes despite the fact that they had almost nothing, made me realize how I give too much importance to material things while there are more things in the world that can bring me so much joy. This is how I learned the concept of living abundantly.

For many, living abundantly usually means living with everything taken care of for you, by your physical attachments. You have a huge closet full of clothes you never wear, gadgets you barely use, and other material things you never really use at all.

According to the dictionary, abundance means overflowing or fullness. Our lives are usually overflowing with different things, and while most of us already have all our basic needs and a little bit more we still don't seem to stop accumulating more and more things. We never become content with what we already have and what's worse, we still complain.

On the other hand, a minimalism lifestyle gives the phrase "abundant life" a positive meaning.

We can live abundantly by aiming for and enjoying things that are not physical. This could mean living a life that is full of love, adventures, peace, purpose, challenge wisdom, comfort, or anything that money couldn't easily buy.

One of the most common clichés we always hear is "live your life". The phrase can mean two different things. First one is to live your life to the fullest, and second, is to do whatever you want without fear. When we're living our lives, we usually experience joy or experience the feeling of harmony or freedom.

But the truth is that whenever we choose to 'live our life to the fullest doing anything we want without fear', we as humans will fill our lives with, material things, things that we think bring us joy, a figment of freedom. This is not how to live abundantly in minimalist perspective; this is living life with anything to make it feel abundant.

I'd say that it's the most difficult part – we are being molded by society to believe that we're living the abundant life with things. And by things, I don't mean only the material things. These things could also be pride, success, or a relationship. This makes you see material things and happiness synonymous – this makes you think that you cannot have life without stuff, just like how you can't have stuff without life.

At first glance, the idea of minimalism may seem contradictory to the word abundance. However, by looking deeper into it, you will realize how abundance and minimalism are actually closely connected – they even go hand-in-hand – in the starting a truly meaningful life.

As minimalists, we're opposed to superfluous excess… Abundance, however, is a totally different thing. The idea behind excess and abundance are the same, certainly, but abundance comes with a deeper definition: "overflowing fullness." I never liked overflowing stuff, but overflowing fullness can possibly be attained by getting rid of some of your stuff. And it's absolutely wonderful.

Starting a habit of getting rid of material things which never served us a purpose can make space for true abundance. We are making an opportunity for overflowing fullness to come into our lives.

In this next part of the book we are going to take a look into three types of abundance that we enjoy by means of embracing minimalism.

Spiritual abundance

Our journey to living a simpler life and embracing the minimalism lifestyle was actually an answered prayer. It started 7 years ago when I lost my job and my wife was about to give birth to our first boy. Desperate, me and my wife and I decided to sell everything we knew we could live without to settle our expenses until I got a job again – after all, all we wanted is to have a good happy life. And when my first child was born, I came to a realization that I am willing to lose everything else in my life, just to make my wife and our child happy. Stuff, and old expectations I had for having "the good life" started flying out the door, and as my physical comforts decreased, my genuine happiness increased.

The following couple of years have been madly stretched and abundant in a spiritual sense. As we have relied less on material things for comfort and depended less on social norm (the idea that a bigger house, more money, the latest devices are important) our contentment has thrived. My wife and I discovered spiritual heights that were buried under all the unnecessary things we thought we had to keep.

Relational abundance

We downsized so that we can pay bills and afford the baby's needs. The driving force behind us to choose to live simpler is so that we can live an abundant life together, as a family. Every single day, I manage to have time to build loving relationships with my wife and my kids. I get to support my wife with her passions, and we're deliberate about making enough time to build on our marriage as well as friendship. Even beyond that, my social circle is richer as I have had the flexibility to meet with my friends and relatives. Deciding to live a simpler life has provided a resilient platform for all these relationships to thrive as it allows me to spend less time and energy on worrying on complete appliances or our smartphones not being the latest model.

Creative abundance

How we see creativity is usually limited to the fine arts: painting, music, sculpture, poetry, song, dance. For me, on the other hand, words are my expression of choice. But even though I've been running my blog for years and I wrote several books as a ghostwriter, I still experience writer's block as finding inspiration can still be a struggle. I set aside some time to have moments of white space each day to allow my soul to breathe, but a lot of times, the creativity that bubbles up out of that beautiful emptiness finds an expression I did not expect. I sing while doing a chore. I doodle on my notebook while on the train. I encourage my kids to try new things that will highlight their creativity. All of these small expressions of creativity carry a delightful joy to my day.

The purpose of minimalism is to release unnecessary things so that truly essential and beautiful things in life can shine through. When you have a lot of things to deal with, managing them all can steal your time, peace of mind, relationship, and creativity. That's something you shouldn't let happen.

Chapter 8

Minimalism Maintenance

Organization and minimalism go hand in hand. Having a well-organized space is in flow with getting rid of the excess, which is an important step to minimalism. However, maintaining it is another thing and something that many people who are trying to live a minimalism lifestyle struggle with.

One of the most common phrases I hear from people who have started to declutter is, "I successfully declutter my space, but after a week or so, my place turned back to how it was." Same things go with the people who tried to change their habits – after a while, they find themselves doing the same things they are trying to get rid of.

Some habits are very difficult to get rid of. They may work for a while, but there is a great chance you go back to the same things you were doing.

Take dieting for example. We always hear from dieticians and nutritionists that a "crash diet doesn't work." This is because this particular way of dieting encourages you to eat less – or skip particular meals – for only a certain period of time until you get rid of the excess weight you want to shed. And while this diet can really be effective in helping you lose weight, there's a big chance that you will regain your weight back, if not, more.

Why does it happen?

This is because the diet encourages you to have a short-term goal, a short-cut to the goal you want to achieve. Okay, say you lose weight for doing the crash diet – you finally reach the weight you wanted, what now? You are likely to celebrate by eating a lot. Eating the food you missed during your diet. Without knowing it, you're slowly getting back to your old habits of eating unhealthy food.

So, how do you actually lose weight?

One of the most effective ways of losing weight and becoming healthy is changing your lifestyle completely. There are types of diet that will allow you to still eat the food you enjoy while making you lose weight and maintain it. Most dieticians suggest a diet that you can stay consistent with for a longer period of time, or even for good – something that will not deprive you from your natural desires and from what your body needs.

The same thing applies when maintaining minimalism. Minimalism is not meant to deprive you of your comfort, but instead, to help you see how living less can also give you comfort in a more meaningful way.

Just like crash dieting, decluttering or minimalism lifestyle, in general, doesn't stop with you, cleaning your place and getting rid of the old stuff you no longer use. It's a lifelong commitment for minimalist, which means, a change of your lifestyle, on the whole, is necessary.

8.1 Ways To Maintain Your Minimalist Lifestyle Permanently

✓ **Be picky about the things you allow in your house**

When you are picky when it comes to what you let inside your house, you're going to facilitate your intentional life. What are the things that are important in your life? What are the things that can really help you improve your life?

Example: If you're running a craft business and it's something you really love to do, it's natural that you'll be needing supplies. Bringing in new supplies for your craft that you need to use is part of your intentional living.

Now, if you're not a crafter and you're considering bringing crafts into your house, then you must reconsider as they are just likely to be clutter to your home.

✓ Be tough when it comes to keeping the clutter out

There's no room for laziness and procrastination when it comes to minimalism. You can save more time and energy by getting rid of all that clutter as soon as you can. Make it a routine to keeping clutter out.

Example: Whenever you finish eating, wash the dishes right away! Don't wait for later or end of the day to come before you deal with them!

✓ Be kind and polite when you refuse something

The world is full of kind and generous people, that I often find myself getting help from even when I don't really need what they're offering.

This is not an excuse to be rude to someone: you can always say no or refuse to accept something without being offensive. Or you can just simply explain to them your lifestyle and recommend giving the help to someone else who may need it more instead.

Example: Your aunt heard that you are planning to move to a new house and so she wants you to get the old sofa they no longer use. You must explain to her that you already have every piece of furniture you need, but that you know of a charity that will gladly accept it.

✓ Be confident in the lifestyle you have chosen

Let's face it…the minimalism lifestyle is not normal.

Although it's gaining popularity today due to its media exposure, it is still not widely followed. I think many people don't realize that they would actually really like minimalism if they gave it a chance. But in today's competitive society it makes it difficult for people not to desire to have better material things to show off, especially where likes and comments on social media become a measuring tool on how we are approved and perceived by others – for some, it's truly addicting.

So, because minimalism would require you to go against the norm of today's society, it's important to stand strong in this lifestyle. You can be kind and understanding to those who don't agree, but you are in no place to change them.

You can be confident that minimalism is a lifestyle that works for you!

Example: Your friend tells you you're weird for being a minimalist. You can just tell him or her that it's the lifestyle that works for you.

Most of the time, there's no point to argue and defend your lifestyle to somebody who's just trying to be rude. Some people just don't understand and it's okay. After all, you're living this lifestyle for you and not for anyone else.

Minimalism lifestyle isn't just a mindless craze. How can it be when it encourages you to make some sort of sacrifice? Generally, those who take steps to simplify and reduce their life, do it because they start to think differently about how they live their lives. Or, they see the wicked and negative nature of inconsiderate consumerism and make a mindful effort to escape this demon within themselves.

Important questions to ask yourself before you bring something new into your house:

Do you really need it?

Is it going to add value to your life?

Will it help you live the life you want?

Do you already have something that does the same purpose?

These questions will keep you from acquiring more things. These are great questions to ask yourself if you are an impulsive shopper and they worked for me 100% of the time.

8.2 Common Items To Never Buy If You Want To Have A Clutter-Free Home

On top of answering the questions mentioned above, knowing exactly the items you must avoid would be one of the best ways to have a clutter-free home – because you know they say… prevention is better than cure. Here are the items you don't want to spend your money on.

Novelty items and seasonal decorations

Today, it's very easy to buy everything you think of… from a serving tray to a wind chime that has seasonal designs. But do you really need them? Getting the novelty versions of daily essentials such as soap dispensers, shower curtains, pillows, bed sheet, and cutlery, restricts their ability to be used all year round. This means they take up storage space the rest of the year when you are not planning to use them. While it might be fun to spend money on a new seasonal item, what's not fun is putting them down to store for the rest of the year. All those festive decoration items become dust-collectors. Before pulling out your wallet, ask yourself, "Is it really worth it to get these decorations for a one-day celebration?"

Trendy clothes

Stop searching for the must-have fashion style of the season. Only because everyone else has a crop top or off-shoulder dresses, doesn't mean you must also have them in your closet. As soon as the fashion trend fades, you will just be left with even more clothes closet to declutter. Rather than following every current trend, choose the clothes you think are flattering for you and something you are comfortable wearing

Kitchen gadgets

All the must-have, single-use, kitchen tools may seem helpful and can make your life easier until you no longer have to use them or they have stopped functioning properly. That is when they're exiled to the brimming gadget drawer that you need to declutter. A smart decluttering tip is to get multi-purpose products. So, avoid getting these kitchen gadgets that aren't worth the money and valuable space.

Organizing solutions

Not many people realize this, but it doesn't mean that because you're buying an organizing solution, you are helping yourself to be organized. In fact, these items may just end up being new clutter. You have to be smart when buying baskets, bins, and boxes as they take up much-needed storage space in your house. Stop storing drawer organizers, containers, label makers, and other solutions. Instead, you may want to focus on trimming down the clutter so there is less stuff you need to store. This way, you won't find the need to get storage solutions.

Trendy cookware

It seems like everyone is starting to own an air fryer. And yes, we still have that popcorn maker we hardly used because cooking popcorn in a pot is also possible.

One of the best things you can do is to resist bringing home the current must-have cookware in the first place. You think you will need them, but chances are, you already have something you in your kitchen you can use as an alternative.

Craft supplies

Bringing home crafting supplies for future crafting projects makes clutter because there's a big chance you'll never follow through on doing the project. Purchasing products to use later, even though you used a discount code or it was in a sale, is just a waste of money. You may just end up forgetting you ever bought it or deciding that you are no longer interested in doing the project. Here is a decluttering tip, whenever you feel crafty, look through your current collection of crafts and get inspiration from there.

"As seen on tv" items

These appealing impulse purchases get to your door in about a couple of weeks, long after the excitement to use them has passed. This just means that they may end up as clutters shoved in your drawer or sitting in the garage. Because it's too expensive to spend money on the return shipping they become one of the harder items to declutter as you paid a lot of money for them and feel guilty just throwing them out. A smart tip to remember is: just don't get them in the first place.

Freebies

And lastly, one of the known culprits for being an instant clutter is the hand-me-downs from well-meant relative, friends, and neighbors. Who doesn't like freebies, though, right? But accepting these will just give you problems later on. Are you really willing to give up storage space for all those things you didn't personally buy?

8.3 Fighting The Desire

Without nurturing the minimalist mindset, minimalism can be a constant battle. You must try to resist temptations around you and reduce both of your physical and mental clutter; you try to look for natural solutions as inner urges build. Just like a crash diet, minimalism without putting your mind to it is likely to end with a big relapse. Pushing against your own desires is a losing battle.

So, if fighting against your own desires isn't what minimalism is all about, then what is it about? I'm in no place to tell you to give up all the things you have for a simpler life. I want to be as realistic as possible and to make your life a little easier. Again, remember that minimalism is about wanting less. You don't have to battle your desires. By knowing these facts, it will be easier for you to maintain this lifestyle.

Conclusion

Hopefully, this book has been helpful to you in understanding what minimalism is. Minimalist lifestyle has a different meaning for different people. But if there's one thing everyone can agree on, it is the fact that minimalism begins in the mind; it is about accepting that we don't need too much. However, it goes past more than just physical items. It goes beyond mindset, health, and even relationships.

Above all else, the best thing about minimalism is the way it benefits a person's emotional state. Rather than feeling tied down and stressed, surrounded by a home that is overflowing with unorganized things, you can embrace minimalism and reorganize your possessions in order or your home to be a place that you truly enjoy spending time in.

The benefits of minimalism can spread into all areas of your life, from decluttering your closet and feeling more organized to letting go of toxic relationships that no longer make you happy.

In many instances, minimalism also brings out the best and worst in humankind. Just look at Black Friday videos that show how modern consumerist standards are just plain wrong. Who cares about your 45-inch flat screen? Is it really worth competing getting yourself in a chaotic situation that can potentially hurt you? Remember that humans were not born to consume and become stuck in a cycle of purchasing stuff in the hopes of raising their social status or filling an emotional void.

At the end of the day, you cannot take material things to your grave — well, technically, you can, but they would not benefit your rotting corpse. So, spend your time on things that are really important in your life.

Similarly, minimalism doesn't need to be followed to the extreme. Minimalism doesn't require you to live in a little white room without belongings and sleep on the floor. More importantly, it is not a competition. For a lot of people, minimalism is the process of striving toward a simpler, more thoughtful lifestyle. Strict devotion to one set of rules, or total self-discipline, isn't required. There are no hard and fast rules.

www.ingramcontent.com/pod-product-compliance
Lightning Source LLC
Chambersburg PA
CBHW031114080526
44587CB00011B/966